Cooking
With Hot Flashes

Books by Martha Bolton

FROM BETHANY HOUSE PUBLISHERS

Didn't My Skin Used to Fit?

I Think, Therefore I Have a Headache!

Cooking With Hot Flashes

Growing Your Own Turtleneck

It's Always Darkest Before the Fridge Door Opens
(with Phil Callaway)

Cooking With Hot Flashes

And Other Ways to Make Middle Age Profitable

MARTHA BOLTON

BETHANYHOUSE
MINNEAPOLIS, MINNESOTA

Cooking With Hot Flashes
Copyright © 2004
Martha Bolton

Cover design by Melinda Schumacher
Cover illustration by Mike Lester

"When I'm an Old Lady," author unknown. Every effort was made to locate source and secure permission.

Published by Bethany House Publishers
11400 Hampshire Avenue South
Bloomington, Minnesota 55438

Bethany House Publishers is a division of
Baker Publishing Group, Grand Rapids, Michigan.

Printed in the United States of America

ISBN-13:   978-0-7642-0002-1
ISBN-10:   0-7642-0002-X

Library of Congress Cataloging-in-Publication Data

Bolton, Martha, 1951-
    Cooking with hot flashes : and other ways to make middle age profitable / by Martha Bolton.
        p.   cm.
    ISBN 0-7642-0002-X (pbk.)
    1. Middle age—Humor. 2. Menopause—Humor. 3. Aging—Humor. I. Title.

PN6231.M47B65   2004
814'.54—dc22

2004012176

After thirty, a body has a mind of its own.
—Bette Midler

MARTHA BOLTON is a full-time comedy writer and the author of over fifty books. She was a staff writer for Bob Hope for fifteen years along with writing for Phyllis Diller, Wayne Newton's USO show, Ann Jillian, Mark Lowry, Jeff Allen, and many others. Her material has appeared in *Reader's Digest, Chicken Soup for the Soul* books, and *Brio* magazine, and she has received four Angel awards and both an Emmy nomination and a Dove Award nomination. Martha and her husband live in Tennessee.

Contents

1

Cooking With Hot Flashes

'Tis not knowing much, but what is useful,
that makes a wise man.
—Thomas Fuller

I'm hot. Not the gorgeous, voluptuous kind of hot. I'm just hot.
My husband tells me I even sizzle. But that is not a compliment. It is simply a statement of fact. I am, at times, quite literally sizzling. So much so that I have been ordered to stay away from dry brush and dead Christmas trees until my body has finished going through this transitional period known as "the change."

The change. Middle age. Menopause. Skin that doesn't fit us anymore. That is just some of what this book is about. But before you men get the misconception that this is a missive intended solely for women, let me remind you that both sexes go through the change. Men just seem to have a lot more fun with it than women. A man wakes up one morning and instead of putting on his usual conservative suit and silk tie, he tosses them both aside, slips on his jeans and unbuttons his shirt to the middle of his chest, adds a couple of gold chains, and goes out and buys a new sports car. That's how the male side of the species faces the midlife transition. For them, it's called a "mid-life crisis," and it's practically a celebration. They begin acting younger, not older. They join health clubs, change their hair-style, their clothes, their demeanor, and their lingo. They get a renewed zest for life. They're not like us. They've never been moved to the smoking section of a restaurant because they were still smoldering from a hot flash. They don't attend weddings just so they can hang around the ice sculpture. They don't sweat puddles every night, so deep they have to wear a life jacket to keep from drowning. The change is easy on them.

But for us women? We can rocket from a normal 98.6-degree body temperature to *volcano* in ten seconds or less. There are veteran firemen who haven't seen that kind of sponta-neous combustion. I'm convinced the only reason any of us get invited to outdoor parties is to serve as the heat lamp.

Perhaps one of these days medical science will develop a thermostat patch for menopausal women that will automatically readjust our body temperature whenever it nears or reaches the boiling point. Who knows, researchers might already be work-ing on this concept even as this book is hitting the bookshelves. I sincerely hope so because when it comes to hot flashes and other symptoms of menopause, we women have suffered far too long in silence!

Oh, all right, who am I kidding? It's never been in silence. If we menopausal women are anything, it's vocal. We know the words "Is it hot in here or is it me?" in twelve languages. We live to let others in on our misery.

"Are you sure Arctic Winter is the lowest setting on your air-conditioner?"

"So, how flexible is cryogenics? Can't I be frozen just until after menopause?"

"That's the third sofa my body has set on fire this week."

We've complained, yes, but until now, we have done little else. We've left it up to the medical community to come up with whatever new and innovative ways they could find to help us handle the uncomfortable, and even dangerous, symptoms of menopause. We haven't done anything significant ourselves to protect us from the symptoms (although flame-retardant pajamas have helped), alleviate our misery, or even find a positive side to menopause. We've never organized a Million Menopausal Woman March on Washington. (What over-forty woman could deal with that kind of claustrophobia?) We haven't spoken out on the floor of Congress. (We figure they've already seen enough uncontrollable crying from the minority party.) As far as I can tell, we haven't done much of anything to make this change of life not only more endurable for us, but perhaps even *financially beneficial.* That is, until now. That is, until *Cooking With Hot Flashes . . . and Other Ways to Make Middle Age Profitable.*

I don't mean to brag, but I believe this book, which is the first to introduce the concept of using hot flashes as an energy source, could quite possibly put me in the running for a Pulitzer or, considering the positive effect it could have on menopausal mood swings, perhaps even a Nobel Peace Prize.

As with many other life-changing discoveries, this hot-flash energy idea came to me quite by accident. One day while clutching a handful of groceries to my chest, I made my way through a crowded supermarket, stood in the checkout line, then continued to cradle the groceries in my arms as I walked home, all the while having one of the worst hot flashes of my life.

But as I was putting the food items away, I noticed something quite remarkable. I discovered that by keeping my groceries pressed against my upper body, my hot flash had apparently cooked a steak to medium and thawed out a bag of frozen peas!

That is what got me to thinking: *I could save a fortune on my gas bill if I just started using my hot flashes to cook with!*

People, this could be the answer to all our energy needs! Who knows? Maybe that's how fire was discovered in the first place. Maybe it wasn't a couple of cavemen rubbing two sticks together as our history books have taught us. Maybe it was a menopausal cave woman who got a hot flash, leaned against her thatched hut, and set it ablaze!

For years scientists have been missing the mark. They've been looking for the answer to the world's power needs in all the wrong places. Since there will never be a shortage of middle-aged women, this natural source of heat energy is virtually unlimited and thus far untapped. Forget building more nuclear power plants. Forget alcohol energy, wind energy, and natural gas energy. Hot-flash energy could be just the discovery to revolutionize the world. Why, just one baby boomer high school reunion could yield enough heat energy to light the entire city of Cincinnati! The possibilities are endless!

But remember, you read it here first. Not in *Newsweek*. Not in *Time*. Not in *Science News*. It was here. A major, world-changing discovery humbly announced within the pages of this book, without a lot of hoopla, without a lot of fanfare (although a couple of oscillating fans pointed in my direction sure would've helped).

Now that I have stepped forward and revealed my discovery to the public, I believe it is only a matter of time before we will be seeing this new source of energy running heavy machinery, automobiles, and even aircraft. The possibilities are limited only by our imagination, our ingenuity, and the intensity of our hot flashes.

Perhaps you are wondering, as I did, why someone has never tapped into this obvious source of energy before now. Excellent question. We women have complained about our hot flashes, comedians have joked about them, pharmaceutical companies have spent hundreds of thousands of dollars trying to bring products to the marketplace that will help alleviate our discomfort, and husbands have gasped at astronomical air-conditioning bills from keeping our houses at a cool and comfortable negative 21 degrees. But even with this much attention, to my knowledge, no one has ever suggested harnessing this natural and abundant source of energy and making it profitable for the world. Maybe we've overlooked it because it seemed too simplistic. Maybe gasoline and electric companies didn't want us discovering such a revolutionary alternative energy source, and their lobbying groups kept us from researching the idea. Maybe we were all just too stinkin' hot to spend that much time in a lab coat. Who knows? It could be any number of reasons.

But since no one else has stepped up to the plate, the duty has fallen to me. So while I await word on my patent application, I figure I might as well go ahead and talk about some of the other ways all of us, men and women alike, can make it through these years known as middle age. Who knows what other solutions to the world's problems are yet to be discovered by studying this passage into the second half of our lives—the time when our muscles might ache a little more, our skin and hair are sure to loosen just a bit, and our knees and opinions won't be bending as easily as they used to. This book is about survival. It's about adventure. It's about discovery. And it should have been about twelve bucks, unless you got it out of the sale bin. In which case, I thank you. It's so embarrassing to walk into a bookstore and find your book hanging out in one of those. So you have my sincere gratitude for rescuing another one.

I hope you enjoy the read, this light-hearted look at our journey into middle age and beyond.

If not, feel free to use it to fan yourself.

I don't deserve this award, but I have arthritis and I don't deserve that either.
—Jack Benny

2

Take Our Money ... Please

*The only reason I made a commercial
for American Express was to pay
for my American Express bill.*
—Peter Ustinov

I don't know about you, but I resent it when advertising companies target younger audiences over older ones. We're just as important, aren't we? We like to spend money, don't we? One look at an outlet mall will tell you, we are a shopping force to be reckoned with.

So why aren't more marketing companies targeting our age group? Why are there so many youth-oriented programs and advertisements on television today? Why are we being ignored? Don't companies realize they are missing a huge market?

Now granted, a visit to the local mall will show you there are a lot of teenagers hanging out there these days. But are they shopping? Are they spending money? No. They're "hanging." Contrary to what our skin might be doing, we members of the over-forty crowd don't "hang." We shop, and not just window shop either. We're serious buyers. When we pick up an item and turn it over to see the price, we often carry it right on over to the checkout counter and pay for it. Why? Because we know the energy involved with picking up items. We don't do it unless we're committed.

If you're still not convinced that middle-agers and seniors are the more dedicated shoppers, then ask yourself this question: *When is the last time you saw a seventeen-year-old pushing one of those little wheeled carts full of packages through a department store?*

I rest my case.

Teenagers don't push wheeled carts. They put whatever they buy in their backpacks or pockets. How much can pockets hold?

Barely anything. Even a backpack is limited. But a wheeled cart has plenty of space, and we are the kings and queens of the wheeled cart. Nothing holds a blanket, a box of Epsom salt, and a bag of prunes better than a wheeled cart. Sure, we may have rolled over a few toes in our rush to a Bluelight Special at Kmart, but the public needs to know that when we are on a mission for bargains, we take no prisoners.

We don't only patronize discount stores, shopping malls, and outlet stores either. We buy from catalogs, television shopping networks, and door-to-door salesmen who are one sale away from winning a trip to the Bahamas. It doesn't matter that we have never been to the Bahamas ourselves, we'll buy whatever we have to in order to help a total stranger get there.

We're trendsetters, too. Do you really think that teenagers

were the ones who started the baggy-pants craze? They weren't. Let me remind you that grandpas have been wearing baggy pants for years. But did clothing manufacturers ever jump on this idea and market the look to Grandpa's age group? Have you ever seen a Calvin Klein commercial with an eighty-year-old shirtless man, wearing pants two sizes too big and hiked up to his armpits, saying "Just be"?

I don't think so. But they took this look and aggressively marketed it to teenagers. Teenagers in their big, baggy pants aren't original. They're not trendsetters. They're just wannabe grandpas.

Another trend that teenagers get credit for starting, but they didn't, is all these wild hair colors. Have they forgotten who it was who started the blue hair trend? Grandmothers. But has one of these lovely ladies ever been offered her own show on MTV? Have they ever been featured on the cover of *Rolling Stone* or *Entertainment Weekly*? Do they get any credit for their hipness?

No. Like Grandpa, their style is copied with no credit given.

But by overlooking the middle-age and senior crowd, advertising executives are missing out on a huge market. Our demographic buys a lot more than just shoe inserts, corn pads, age-defying face creams, and support hose. We buy toys and computer games for our grandchildren, nieces, nephews, friends' children, and yes, even for ourselves sometimes. We buy clothes and household goods, computers and compact discs (even though the word disc makes us a little nervous). We buy high-ticket items, low-ticket items, and everything in between. Contrary to what you may think, limited budget doesn't mean broke. We'll spend, but we just want a good value for our money.

We buy furniture, clothes, makeup, purses, shoes, carpets, vacuum cleaners, ride-on lawn mowers, hot-water heaters, cars, and major appliances. You won't find all that on a teenager's shopping list.

We also pay for household repairs, patronize hair salons, restaurants (both fast-food and fine dining), and we go on trips (not just cruises or road trips in our Winnebagos; many of us still take business trips).

So why then aren't the marketing people targeting our demographic more often? Young professionals may make more money than us annually, but they've got $4.98 in their savings account. We may make less than they do, but we have substantially more in our savings accounts to spend. I myself am up to nine dollars now.

I suppose it will take a while to change the thinking of these advertising executives, so we'll have to be patient. In the meantime, we'll just have to continue doing what we've done all along: shop. Spend our money. And keep watching all those Calvin Klein commercials with their "hip" teenagers modeling those baggy britches, knowing all along that Grandpa could be doing a much better job.

You can tell the ideals of a nation
by its advertisements.
—Norman Douglas

3

Exercising Our Prerogative

I burned sixty calories. That should take care
of a peanut I had in 1962.
—Rita Rudner

They say our metabolism slows down during middle age. Mine
didn't just slow down. It pulled over and parked. No matter
what I do, I can't seem to get it to shift into gear and take to
the road again. It's perfectly content to sit there on the shoulder
of life's highway and watch the world go by. Meanwhile, every
morsel that I eat attaches itself to my frame and hangs on like a
barnacle on the Queen Mary.

The answer? Some say it's exercise. Regular exercise is supposed to increase the body's metabolism and help it burn off all
those extra calories that we happen to take in throughout our
day.

But I for one have never been very fond of exercise. I have
enough night sweats, why would I want to sweat during the
day, too?

Exercising with exercise equipment holds the least appeal for me. Sure, the TV ads make the rowing machines and various other equipment look easy. You don't see anyone huffing and puffing and begging for oxygen. The spokespeople simply do their workout, pat their cheeks and foreheads with a hand towel, and tell you how much it will cost (plus shipping and handling) to have one of their miracle machines in the privacy of your home.

Now, I might find working out on exercise equipment a little more tempting if there was more of an incentive than merely losing weight. If I'm going to work that hard on a machine, I want something worthwhile at the other end of all my stretching. In other words, I'd gladly do the Gazelle or the AB Slide if there was a box of Krispy Kremes just slightly out of my reach. I'd have no problem at all walking a treadmill if there was a hot fudge sundae staring back at me from the opposite end of the conveyor belt. Real incentives, that's what I need. Merely visualizing myself in a pair of size–8 jeans isn't enough anymore. I need tangible rewards, rewards I can see, feel, and cover with whipped cream and nuts.

Exercise videos and television programs don't motivate me either. I don't like all the yelling.

"Get off that sofa and get moving!" the trainer will bark.

Now, first of all, I'm not usually sitting on the sofa. I'm laid out on the recliner. There is a difference. And secondly, why can't she ask nicely? When you're already so out of shape that one sit-up takes half the afternoon, who wants a drill sergeant making you feel bad about it? The way I see it is, if someone wants me to twist and bend my body into contortions that have never before been seen or imagined, there had better be a "pretty please" attached.

I don't know about you, but I don't need any more guilt. I already feel guilty enough every time I take my fork up to the dessert bar at the buffet and skip the plate. (Okay, like nobody else has ever thought of doing that?)

And anyway, it's not like I don't get any exercise at all. I walk to my mailbox every day, and on some days I have had to look all over the family room for the remote, and who knows how many steps I take doing that? I do knee bends getting the Fritos that I keep on the bottom shelf of the cupboard and shoulder stretches reaching up for the Breyers in the top freezer. I'd like to see someone come out with a video featuring these kinds of exercises.

But I'm not completely convinced we should be burning all these calories, anyway. How do we know it's a good thing? Has anyone ever researched where all these burned calories are going and what they might be doing to our environment? What if burned calories are, in fact, what's messing up the ozone layer? What if it isn't hair spray at all? What if one day we discover that calories are something we were supposed to keep with us, not go sending off willy nilly into the atmosphere?

Until more research is done on exactly where all these spent calories are going and how the loss of them is affecting our world, I choose to limit my incineration of the little guys. It's not that I'm lazy. I'm patriotic. Wait, no, it's more than patriotism. This is a much higher calling. This has global significance. This could be yet another world-changing idea. I shall clear space in my office for my second Pulitzer. And I shall set an example to all others by vowing to burn only a handful of calories every day. It's the very least I can do to save our world.

> *Whenever I feel like exercise I lie down*
> *until the feeling passes.*
> —Robert M. Hutchins

4

I Left My Chin in Ol' Zimbabwe

I've had more parts lifted
than an abandoned Mercedes.
—Phyllis Diller

The latest marketing angle for plastic surgery is the combined surgery/safari trip. Have you heard about these? You go on a safari in some faraway land and get your face lifted at the same time. Imagine it—bagging some wild game and getting rid of a few under-eye bags at the same time. How convenient is that?

The theory behind mixing these two activities, I suppose, is so that the recovery will be discreet. Elephants don't care whether or not your stitches are showing, and who's a giraffe going to blab your face-lift secret to?

After the safari and operation, you simply return to your homeland looking twenty years younger and no one is the wiser.

Another activity that is growing in popularity is the Botox home party. From what I understand, you invite some of your closest friends over and a doctor explains the benefits of Botox, and then he or she will give Botox injections to whomever wants them and is deemed a good candidate for them. It's like a Tupperware party, only you and your guests are the ones trying to lock in your freshness.

Times have sure changed, haven't they? I remember the day when plastic surgery was something people only whispered about.

"Do you think she's had any work done?"

"Please, she's gone through more cuts than a Republican budget."

But these days, there are no whispers. The people themselves brag about what they've had done. It's like they consider themselves walking works of art.

"That's a Dr. Carter nose, isn't it? I recognize his style."

"Actually, it's a Doc Sheridan. He's a little more impressionistic than I'd like, but I suppose I'll eventually get used to both of my eyebrows being on the same side."

These days, celebrities, politicians, and even everyday people have no problem confessing their nips, tucks, reductions, and enhancements. They're proud of them.

A few celebrities, however, have proven that too much of a good thing can have undesirable results. I don't have to name names, because I think you have a good idea of whom I'm talking about. They've had so much plastic surgery, they don't look real anymore. They're like caricatures of themselves. It's sad, but at this point, I don't know if there's anything they can do about it. They've reached the point of no return. They can't be very happy about that either. But it's not all their fault. Where were their friends? Where was their family? Where was their doctor? Where was someone, anyone, who could have said to them, "Look, I love you, but your nose is starting to invert. You gotta stop, man"?

A plastic surgery intervention was desperately needed.

Don't get me wrong. I'm not against plastic surgery. But everything should be done in moderation. People shouldn't go through a dozen different noses before they find one they like. This isn't Silly Putty they're working with; it's flesh and bone and cartillage. If you've already had a successful experience with plastic surgery, I'm happy for you. All I'm saying is know when to stop. And if you've never had plastic surgery but are contemplating getting some work done, I would simply say to talk to your doctor and your family and do whatever you believe is best for you.

And if that involves going on a safari, then do it. Or if it means staying just the way you are, that's great, too. The important thing is to just be you.

Wrinkles should merely indicate
where the smiles have been.
—Mark Twain

5

They're Out to Rule the World

There was no respect for youth when I was young, and now that I am old, there is no respect for age—I missed it coming and going.
—J. B. Priestly

The kids are taking over. I'm not talking about all the doctors, policemen, politicians, and attorneys who seem to be getting younger and younger each year. I'm talking about children. Real children. More specifically, toddlers. They could be your nieces and nephews, your grandchildren, your neighbors' kids, or in some cases, even your own children. And sure, they seem innocent enough sitting there in their cribs or on the floor playing quietly with their toys, but it's all a ruse. They have an agenda, they're committed, and they've been outsmarting us for years. Everything they do is to advance their plan to take over the world, and it's high time someone blew their cover.

And so I shall.

This plan of theirs has been unfolding ever so subtly over the years. Even I didn't suspect anything was amiss at first. But I see it all quite plainly now.

First, I'm not sure how they did it, but somehow these little rug rats have managed to take over the control of our television sets. Instead of watching our favorite news programs or the History Channel, we find ourselves caving in to their desires and watching *SpongeBob* and *Jimmy Neutron* for hours on end. Granted, we do get involved in the programs and even catch ourselves laughing out loud sometimes, but has anyone played their theme songs backward to see if they're sending subliminal messages to the adult world?

"You will let me play ball in your house."

"You will take me to Chuck E. Cheese's."

"You will give me an advance on my inheritance."

"You will let me braid your hair in tiny little braids and paint your toenails fluorescent pink."

Who knows what kind of adult brainwashing is going on during these seemingly innocent children's shows?

The television was just Phase 1 of the master plan. Phase 2 apparently happened while many of us middle-agers and seniors were taking naps. These innocent-looking children somehow convinced pharmaceutical companies of the need for our medicine bottles to come with childproof caps. Caps, I might add, that only *children* can open. Now, on the surface, childproofing medicine bottles probably sounded like a great idea, and I do not doubt for a minute that the staff at the Federal Drug Administration had plenty of reputable data to convince the agency to jump on board with this seemingly beneficial plan. But the FDA should have been a tad more skeptical. They weren't looking into the future and seeing where this action was taking us as a society. Adults are now at the mercy of children!

"I need my heart medication, Joey," Grandpa says. *"Can you come over here and get this blasted thing open for me?"*

"Sure, Gramps, as soon as you reveal the password to your safety deposit box."

These children are the same ones who also hide our glasses, our car keys, our wallets, the *TV Guide,* and then merely giggle, clam up, or speak some kind of gibberish when we try to interrogate them about the missing items.

"Where are my keys, Bobby?"

"Ahgagoga."

"Come on, boy, tell Nana where you put them."

"Dimofogu."

Their resistance to these inquisitions would impress military experts worldwide. Both the FBI and the CIA have tried to decipher their secret code, but it's unbreakable.

We're headed for trouble, people.

And who is it that gets the power seat at the dinner table? The "high" chair? (See, even the name sounds commanding.) Who is responsible for that incessant pounding on the metal trays that would make even the toughest grandparent shout out every password to every account he's ever owned? These toddlers, that's who.

Remember the good ol' days when children used to be at the mercy of adults when it came to their mobility? They either rode in a stroller or we carried them. That, too, has changed.

These days, kids have their own battery-operated cars to putt around in. They're eighteen months old and already they know how to drive. What's worse, we're probably the ones they persuaded to buy these vehicles for them.

Which brings us to their incredible business sense. These youngsters are nothing short of financial geniuses. Think about it. They come to our houses selling candy for their schools and youth organizations, then they return on Halloween and take it all back! Has anyone done the math on this?

I'm telling you, world, their hostile takeover has been planned right under our noses and we've been too blinded by their cuteness to see it. They've been holding high-level security meetings in sandboxes all over the globe. Sure, it all looks like innocent play to us, but it isn't. It's their own version of Camp David. Why do you think there's always one child who holds that ear-piercing high-pitched scream? You think it's a tantrum? I used to think that, too. But no longer am I that naïve. The scream is a cover-up so we won't overhear them discussing their takeover plans.

These toddlers have their own cell phones, computers, playhouses, and miniature emergency vehicles. What do they need us big people for? They've got almost everything required to run the world on their own.

The most amazing thing about this is how these little ones have managed to get us to run their publicity campaigns for them, and we've been doing it *pro bono*.

"You wanna see some pictures of the most beautiful grandchild on earth?"

"You think she's beautiful, wait 'til you see my grandbaby!"

We're ready to play dueling grandchildren at the drop of a photo album.

"Look at those eyes!"

"Look at those dimples!"

"He's the smartest kid in the world!"

So, all things considered, maybe we're just getting what we deserve. These little ones have been outsmarting us for years, manipulating us with their cute smiles and endearing hugs, while we've merely sat by and allowed it all to happen.

But it's not too late. We must wake up and smell the apple juice in the sippee cup. The future of the world is at stake! No matter how cute they are, we cannot continue to roll over and let these kids take over. We can't bury our heads and pretend we don't know what they're up to. It's time we quit being weak! It's time we stood up and drew a line in their sandboxes! It's time we let them know once and for all who's in charge here! It's time we . . .

Sorry. This chapter was going to be a lot longer, but a two-year-old in my doctor's waiting room just took my glasses and won't give them back, so I can't see my laptop keys.

And so the conspiracy continues. . . .

True terror is to wake up one morning and discover that your high school class is running the country.
—Kurt Vonnegut

6

The Fountain of Youth Uncovered

*I am my age. I'm not making
any effort to change it.*
—Harrison Ford

I seriously doubt if there really is a fountain of youth, but I think I might have stumbled across what could very well be the next best thing.

One day while surfing the Internet, I came across a rather interesting tidbit of information. I read that a can of WD–40 spray can be useful in the treatment of arthritis. I had never heard that before, and quite frankly, I don't even know if the claim is true or not. The manufacturer might not even be aware that someone is making this claim. But according to the information I uncovered, all you do is rub a little of the popular lubricant onto the affected area, and before you know it, you're doing cartwheels down the hallway.

As I said, I have my doubts about whether this really works, but it did get me thinking. What else might be lurking in our garages that can help us get through the second half of our lives? Could it be that the fountain of youth has been hiding out there all these years, while we've been searching the world over for it? Could it be that Craftsman can do us more good than anti-aging creams? Could Home Depot be the secret location of Shangri-La?

Who knows? But I figured it was worth checking out. So I walked into my garage and took a look around to see what I could find.

The first item to catch my eye was our Weedwacker. Could that be the perfect tool for trimming those pesky ear and nose hairs? Traditionally, the Weedwacker has been used for bigger jobs, but if you let ear hair growth go unchecked for a few weeks, the Weedwacker might be just the thing to tackle an unruly hedge or two.

Sandpaper is another garage tool that might be able to help us look younger. Why should we continue to mess around with goopy masques and toning creams just trying to get rid of all our dead skin cells? Why not sandpaper them off instead? Sandpaper is cheaper and can reach depths in our pores we never thought possible. (For those more difficult places such as elbows and heels, the electric sander might be able to work miracles, but we should each check with our own doctor first.)

Many of us have tried virtually everything to get rid of cellulite, but we haven't tried putty! Putty might be just the thing to fill in all those potholes and smooth out our legs again. If that doesn't work, we could try that Pops-a-Dent device. You know, the one they advertise on television that pops the dents right out of your car's fenders. It seems to me if it can do that, maybe it can fix cellulite, too. In other words, pull the "sink" right out of the "sinkholes."

The last garage tool that I'm going to mention, although I'm sure there are plenty more, happens to be the most versatile one, too. Duct tape. For those of us who can't afford an expensive plastic surgeon, duct tape might very well be our answer. It's affordable, easily accessible, and convenient to use. You can tape back loose skin, reinforce falling body parts, and who knows what else? It comes in colors now, too, so whatever your skin tone, whether you have blond, brunette, red, or black hair, there's a color just right for you.

Or on second thought, maybe it would be better if we all just got out of our garages and stuck with products that have already been proven to minimize the signs of aging. Bob Vila is busy enough without all of us showing up at his garage wanting makeovers!

*There is a fountain of youth: it is your mind,
your talents, the creativity you bring to your
life and the lives of the people you love.
When you learn to tap this source,
you will truly have defeated age.*
—Sophia Loren

7

The Ultimate Word on Aging

*When I told my doctor I couldn't afford an
operation, he offered to touch-up my X-rays.*
—Henry Youngman

With all the books being marketed today on the subject of
aging, you wouldn't think that some of the best advice on this
subject would come from one of the oldest books around—the
Bible. That's right. Even the heroes of the faith had to deal with
many of the same problems that we face today, and they even
wrote about it.

Just take a look at what we can learn from this "over forty"
crowd of the scriptures. (By the way, I'm using the version of
the Bible that's considered by the majority of theologians to be
the most authentic. Large print.)

So what does the Bible say about aging?

✿ **Sometimes even kings can't seem to get warm.**
*When King David was old and well advanced in years, he
could not keep warm even when they put covers over him.*
—1 Kings 1:1

✿ **Exercising, even if it's just walking around in circles, can keep you healthy.**

Moses was a hundred and twenty years old when he died, yet his eyes were not weak nor his strength gone.

—Deuteronomy 34:7

✿ **To dye or not to dye.**

The glory of young men is their strength, gray hair the splendor of the old.

—Proverbs 20:29

✿ **Even bald can be beautiful.**

When a man has lost his hair and is bald, he is clean.

—Leviticus 13:40

✿ **You deserve to be heard.**

Moses was eighty years old and Aaron eighty-three when they spoke to Pharaoh.

—Exodus 7:7

✿ **. . . but don't ramble.**

Seated in a window was a young man named Eutychus, who was sinking into a deep sleep as Paul talked on and on. When he was sound asleep, he fell to the ground from the third story and was picked up dead.

—Acts 20:9

✿ **Don't get stuck in your ways.**

Better a poor but wise youth than an old but foolish king who no longer knows how to take warning.

—Ecclesiastes 4:13

✿ **The older you get, the more you deserve respect.**

Listen to your father, who gave you life, and do not despise your mother when she is old.

—Proverbs 23:22

✿ **Insomnia is curable.**

I will lie down and sleep in peace, for you alone, O LORD, make me dwell in safety.

—Psalm 4:8

✿ **God's not through with you yet.**

They will still bear fruit in old age, they will stay fresh and green . . .

—Psalm 92:14

✿ **You are not alone.**

Even to your old age and gray hairs I am he, I am he who will sustain you. I have made you and I will carry you; I will sustain you and I will rescue you.

—Isaiah 46:4

✿ **And you are not forgotten.**

Abraham was now old and well advanced in years, and the LORD had blessed him in every way.

—Genesis 24:1

✿ **Geritol's good, but God is better.**

He will renew your life and sustain you in your old age.

—Ruth 4:15

✿ **And never ever say never.**
After Noah was 500 years old, he became the father of Shem, Ham and Japheth.

—Genesis 5:32

My secret for staying young is good food, plenty of rest, and a makeup man with a spray gun.
—Bob Hope

8

Another Fine Mess

Try to relax and enjoy the crisis.
—Ashleigh Brilliant

I fully understand the importance of airport security. In these times in which we live, it has become an accepted part of life. So I didn't mind at all when I had to comply with some of these security measures when my rhinestone-sleeved sweater recently set off the alarm at a Missouri airport.

You know the routine. As soon as I walked through the security scanner, it started beeping. A guard politely asked me to step to the side, and of course I did. He asked me to stretch out both of my arms. I did that, too. He asked me to spread my legs. I did that as well. I went along with the routine even though I had a pretty good hunch as to what the problem might be.

"It's the rhinestones," I said as he waved his security wand down and around my right arm. "I'm sure it's the rhinestones."

The guard didn't seem very interested in my assessment of

the situation. He merely indicated that I should stay still and stay quiet while he continued.

There was no beeping on my right arm, so he moved on, waving the wand down and around my left arm. But there was no beeping with my left arm either. Next, he scanned my legs. Nothing. My shoulders. Nothing. My head, an even eerier silence. I waited for him to comment about that, but they're not allowed to joke around.

Then the silence was broken.

Beep, beep, beep, beep . . .

He had moved the wand in the vicinity of my lower back.

Aha. There was the problem. But what could it be? I asked myself. There wasn't anything in my lower back area that should be setting off the alarm.

He moved his wand up to my shoulder area. The beeping stopped. He waved it around my hip area. Nothing. Then he moved it back down to my lower back and around to the front of my stomach area, and . . .

Beep, beep, beep . . .

There was no question about it. He had found the problem area.

"It's here," he said emphatically. "There's something under here."

Of course there was something under there. It was my stomach. But it shouldn't have been triggering a security alarm. I don't eat *that* much iron. But I didn't say that, remembering the no-joking-around rule.

"What've you got under there?" he asked.

"Nothing," I said.

"Nothing?"

"There's nothing there," I said confidently.

"You wearing a belly ring?"

Right, I laughed to myself. AARP was running a special. But I didn't say that either.

"No. No belly ring," I assured him.

"Belt?"

"No."

"Metal plates?"

"I could probably use a few, but no."

All right, I didn't say that either. These kinds of situations are very difficult for humor writers. But I realized that it wasn't the time or the place, so I edited myself.

The guard wanded me again, just to double check, and once again everywhere was silent except for my lower torso.

Beep, beep, beep, beep, beep. The alarm was insistent. Something was there.

"I don't know what it could be," I insisted. And I honestly didn't. I had already mentally surveyed my body. There wasn't anything there that should have been causing all this commotion.

The guard felt around my waistline one more time.

"There's something here, ma'am. Feels like some sort of fanny pack. You got a fanny pack under there?" he pressed.

"No."

"Then what's under there?"

"Just my stomach," I repeated. If my stomach felt like a fanny pack to him, I was sure there was a better way for him to have worded that. But again, my lips were sealed.

Other guards were starting to move in closer now as backup.

"What's the problem?" one of them asked, sizing me up.

"Something keeps triggering my wand," he said.

A suspicious glance was exchanged between the guards, while my mind reviewed my body once more from head to toe. No belt. No metal plates. No belly ring. No fanny pack. There was nothing that should have been setting off any alarms. And yet it was.

Beep, beep, beep, beep.

Just as I was envisioning the nightly news featuring my picture, it suddenly dawned on me. In the hustle and bustle to get to the airport, the girdle that I don't always wear but had decided to wear that day because the skirt I was wearing seemed to scream for it had bunched itself up into a tiny roll that I had told myself I was going to fix once I got on the plane. Never figuring a girdle in any condition would trigger the alarm system, I had forgotten all about it.

But because it had bunched up into a roll, the metal stays must have appeared on the X ray to be two or three times thicker than a normal girdle and were now sounding all sorts of alarms.

I leaned over and discreetly whispered to the guard that I thought I knew what the problem might be. I explained the rolled-girdle theory, he felt the bulk again, then concurred with my assessment.

"It's just a girdle!" he explained to the other guards and also to the crowd of people who had now gathered, curiously staring at the group inspection of my midsection.

"It bunched up," he said, relieved that his duties were done and the crisis of the moment had been successfully averted.

I could hear a few snickers as I waited for the boarding process to begin, and I believe I heard the word "girdle" spoken in Spanish, French, and Japanese. A few school-age kids pointed, and I think I saw the pilots receiving a briefing before boarding the plane.

When I finally stepped onto the plane myself, I walked straight to the airplane lavatory and took off that trouble-causing body tourniquet. It wasn't easy, considering the small space I had to do it in. I accidentally rang the flight attendant three times and turned on the faucet with my right hip. But after tugging and pulling, pulling and tugging, I was free at last! It felt great. I could breathe again. And I could rest assured that I wouldn't be setting off any more airport alarms.

To tell you the truth, I don't even know why I was wearing that crazy thing in the first place. Considering what I had paid for my airline tickets, wasn't that enough of a squeeze?

In youth we run into difficulties.
In old age difficulties run into us.
—Beverly Sills

9

Brain-Aerobics

*Ever wonder if illiterate people
get the full effect of alphabet soup?*
—John Mendosa

A recent medical report stated that the simple act of juggling helps to keep the middle-aged brain alert. So, I've been doing a lot of that lately. I've been juggling my mortgage, my car payment, my utilities, and my credit card payments. I haven't noticed any significant difference in my brain power, but my head does seem to be hurting a lot more.

This same report also said that getting plenty of sleep can rejuvenate the mind and improve reflex time. I don't think I believe that either. The other day I woke up from a wonderful nap just in time to see that I was about to drive right off the road. It still took my reflexes a good five or six seconds to kick in. Frankly, I don't see where that nap helped me very much at all.

Another activity that is reported to be good for our brains is working crossword puzzles. I'm not sure if it is the act of completing the puzzle, or if it's just all that hunting around for a pencil that helps to stimulate our brain waves.

One look at the spam in our e-mail in-boxes will tell you that there certainly is no shortage of products on the market that guarantee (and I use the term loosely) to improve our brainpower in middle age. The subject lines vary, but each company seems to be playing to this same basic desire. We want our brains to stay as young and healthy as possible for as long as possible.

Personally, I don't get caught up in all this hype because I'm pretty sure my brain is going to outlast my body. My body clearly has had more wear and tear on it than my brain. The reason for this is that over the years I've purposely endeavored to keep my brain in relatively new condition, only using it on special occasions.

When my mother was alive she used to say that certain foods were "brain foods." Hot oatmeal fell into this category. She may have been right. Oatmeal does make you feel smarter. Especially when you realize you just paid around a buck for a box of it, as opposed to four dollars for a box of cereal.

My mother never told me this, but I've wondered if cheesecake isn't brain food, too. Here's my theory. Many say that the best cheesecake is New York cheesecake. New York is home of the Metropolitan Museum of Art, Columbia University, Cornell University, and the New York City Opera.

See the connection?

Let's try "patty melt." A patty melt is made with sourdough bread. San Francisco is famous for sourdough. San Francisco is home to the San Francisco Law School and the de Young Art Museum.

Chicago-style pizza? Chicago has Northwestern University and the Chicago Arts District.

Baked Alaska? The University of Alaska Museum.

Tennessee Tea Cakes? Vanderbilt University.

The way I see it, oatmeal isn't the only food that is good for our brains. There are plenty of other desserts, entrees, and deep-fried appetizers that could very well increase your brain power. Boston Cream Pie (Boston University and Harvard Medical School), Texas chili (Texas A&M), California nacho cheese (Berkeley, USC, and UCLA), Kentucky Fried Chicken (University of Kentucky). I could go on, but I believe I've made my point.

So whether it's vitamins, brain exercises, or even my list of "brain foods," the important thing is that we do something every day to nourish and stimulate our minds.

Tonight I'm having Tiramisu and canolis. Obviously, I'm studying abroad.

You are the same today that you are going to be five years from now except for two things: the people with whom you associate and the books you read.
—Charles Jones

Ten Things You Don't Realize Until Middle Age

✿ Good posture was a good idea.

✿ When given a choice, downhill is the preferred direction.

✿ No matter how big you get, you never outgrow naps.

✿ The Weather Channel is great television.

✿ As long as your car's left-turn signal is keeping time with your car radio, there is no need to turn off either one.

✿ It doesn't matter how long you live, you will never go through all the hot-sauce packets you've been given at Taco Bell.

✿ Pants really do seem to fit better when they're pulled up to your armpits.

✿ Some mornings facial concealer should come with a roller.

✿ Chocolate isn't a food group. It's a whole diet plan.

✿ Sometimes pantyhose just aren't worth the fight.

11

It's Not Just the Economy That's Sagging

I am a fighter. Gravity is my enemy.
—Gertrude Schwartz

A few years ago, I moved to the South. So did my body. In fact, there are several parts of me that have relocated to the deep south.

I'm not sure why, but gravity seems heavier in middle age than it did when I was younger. And therein lies the problem. You may not believe this, but gravity has gained weight. I'm still working on how to go about proving this, but I'm convinced it's true. Just ask yourself, is it harder for you to get up from a sitting position these days? Is it harder for you to climb out of bed in the morning? Is it harder for you to hold your head and shoulders back? If the answer is "yes," don't be discouraged. It's not you. It's gravity. Gravity keeps gaining weight and we just can't go on lifting it up anymore.

Gravity's weight gain is the reason behind the little flesh avalanches my body has been having lately. I'm convinced of it. These are parts of me that have stood faithfully at their posts decade after decade. There wasn't a deserter among them. But now, these same parts have begun to give me the slip.

Take my eyebrows as just one example. Before hitting middle age, they used to sit firmly above my eyes. They were happy there. They didn't have any real complaints. They didn't shift to the right or to the left. They didn't slide down or move over. They stayed perfectly in place, right where God originally designed them to be. Not once did I have to give them a second thought.

But something happened to them once I hit middle age. They let go, surrendered; they hoisted the white flag. They had held on for as long as they could, then simply gave up. They served me well, but they have now gone AWOL. At the present moment, both of my eyebrows are drooping down so low in front of my eyes, I can pluck them without using a mirror. Whenever I work at my computer now, I have to tilt my head back just to keep them from slamming down on my keyboard. I can't write this way. I need to see what letters I'm tyzyping. (Sorry, that should have been "typing." See what I mean?)

But I can't put all the blame on my eyebrows. The little troopers have simply succumbed under the expanding weight of gravity.

A lot of me has given up and let go lately. In addition to my eyebrows, my cheeks have suffered substantial slippage, too, thanks to the added weight of the g-word. My cheeks used to have a firm grip on my facial bones, but not anymore. Now they're hanging down like the jowls of a Saint Bernard. Even the best glamour photo can't be touched up enough to hide something like that.

Every day I wonder what body part will become the latest casualty in this seemingly uncontrollable flesh avalanche. I'm dropping faster than the interest rates of 2003. I feel like a Mrs. Potato Head being rearranged by someone with a cruel sense of humor who's playing around with all the parts, putting them in places they've never been before and do not belong.

Without a doubt, gravity has had the biggest effect on my skin. To put it bluntly, my skin has been my downfall. Menopausal skin is like pantyhose that start out at your waist in the morning and work their way down to your ankles by noon. You end up looking like you're wearing slouch socks when you're not.

But there's not a lot we can do about any of this. Gravity is well past its middle age. If it's going to gain weight, this is the time that it would be happening. Still, it makes you wish that we would have been handed some sort of a warranty at our birth, something that would cover us in middle age when we begin suffering significant body-part movement. Our homes are covered for foundation slippage. Why not our bodies? When you think about it, it's not that far-fetched a concept. Both Betty Grable and Mary Hart had their legs insured for a million dollars. Others have insured different parts of their bodies, too. Why couldn't there be a Skin Slippage clause or a Falling Eyebrows Indemnity policy?

Another life-changing idea from just one middle-aged

author. I'm going to have to buy a bigger house just to display all the Nobels.

But I'm afraid until Lloyd's of London or State Farm or some other insurance company finds a way to make this kind of policy affordable for everyday people, it'll have to remain just another good idea. We'll have to deal with the damages caused by Flesh Falls all on our own, and try our best not to trip over our ankles.

> *Old age is like a plane flying through a storm.*
> *Once you're aboard, there's nothing you can do.*
> —Golda Meir

12

The Sandman Cometh . . . But He Delayeth

Waking up in the morning would be a whole lot easier if it involved flopping into bed, burying my head into my pillow, and closing my eyes.
—Jeffery D. Trock

Maybe it's just me, but it seems that once we enter the middle-age years, we don't get or require as much sleep as we once did. One reason for this could be the fact that at our age there are a lot more fun things to do in bed. Now, I'm not talking about the obvious (shaking your spouse and telling him or her to "Roll over, you're snoring again"). I'm talking about all those *other* fun things to do.

For instance, when we were children, all we had to count before drifting off to sleep was a bunch of imaginary sheep jumping over a fence. How boring was that? But now that we're older, we can lie in bed and count floaters! (If you don't know what floaters are, they're those little black things that float across your field of vision every now and then, and they seem to get more prominent in middle age.) Once floaters have been deemed harmless by your opthalmologist, they can really be quite entertaining. Especially at bedtime. Simply lie back on your pillow and follow the path of one until it floats out of sight, then pick up on another one just as it enters your field of vision. Do this for a few minutes, and before you know it, you're snoozing like a baby. Or you're permanently cross-eyed.

Another fun thing to do in bed is what I call The Blanket Tuck. With this game, timing is everything. The tuck has to be perfectly timed to occur just prior to your spouse's rolling over. Being as discreet as possible, tuck the blanket under the side of your body closest to the outer edge of the bed. You want to make sure that it is a tight tuck, as tight as you can get it. Then, when your spouse tries to roll over, he or she will move, but the blanket won't. Imagine the playful giggles the two of you will share as you enjoy this little game together.

"Give me the covers!"

"You give me the covers!"

"Give me the covers!"

"You give me the covers!"

Why, you'll feel like newlyweds again.

Another fun activity to play in bed is Mattress Ice Skating. This involves simply moving your bare feet in a circular motion around your partner's icy toes and pretending you're skating. For extra enjoyment, try a few figure eights.

Reading is another activity to do in bed, but not just the warning label on your pillows. That's fun, too, but I'm talking books. My husband loves to read in bed, which I believe has been the reason for much of our closeness. He likes to read big, thick history books that tend to make his side of the bed sag. This causes me to roll over to his side of the bed and he thinks I'm being romantic.

I love to write in bed. Over the years, I've found that some of my best ideas come to me in the middle of the night. I also know that if I don't write them down, I'll forget them by morning. So I grab a pen and paper in the dark and scribble down all the important points of my idea. It could be an idea for a book, a screenplay, a song, or a sketch. Whatever happens to come into my mind, I'll jot it down.

In the morning I can't read a word of it. Before I became a writer, I had no idea that between the hours of 2 and 4 A.M., I'm bilingual.

I'm sure there are plenty of other fun things to do in bed during your middle-age years, but this should give you a few tips to start with. And just remember, if you really get bored, you can always go back to doing that other thing you used to do when you were a whole lot younger.

Sleep.

I usually take a two-hour nap from one to four.
—Yogi Berra

13

Not by a Hair on
My Chinny Chin Chin

*I refuse to think of them as chin hairs.
I think of them as stray eyebrows.*
—Janette Barber

When we women hit middle age, we start wishing for something that will hide our wrinkles. A beard is the last thing on our minds.

What is it about menopause that makes the hair on our heads start letting go, while the hair on our faces seems to sprout overnight like Jack's beanstalk? Has anyone come up with a good explanation for this? We hear so much about mysterious crop circles popping up in wheat fields overnight; but to my knowledge, no one is investigating where all these chin hairs are coming from. Isn't their sudden nocturnal appearance every bit as puzzling? I can go to bed with a nice smooth chin, and by morning I look like I should be baaing. This is not normal.

These hairs are often not even the same color as the hair on the rest of our bodies, which makes them appear even more mysterious. But did you ever see an episode of *The X-Files* dedicated to the sudden materialization of chin hairs? Has *Unsolved Mysteries* ever covered this unexplained phenomenon? Or *60 Minutes* aired an exposé?

To my knowledge, the answer is no. So once again, I'm taking it to the public myself. Put the crop circle mystery on hold. Bigfoot and the Loch Ness Monster are going to have to wait. We middle-agers have been left to twirl our chin hair long enough while pondering this conundrum. We want answers and we want them now. Where is Morley Safer when we need him? Agent Fox Mulder, report back for duty. Robert Stack, look into this problem for the good of your country. We demand to know what possible reason there could be for this spontaneous chin-hair growth on menopausal women. Is it so our grandchildren will have something to hang on to when they climb into our laps? Is it so we'll be able to tell which way the wind is blowing on any given day? Is it to save us a fortune on dental floss? What possible purpose could there be for this enigma?

We have been patient long enough. We have tried handling these mystery hairs on our own. We've shaved or plucked them, but it still doesn't deter them in the least. They simply grow back, and when they do, it's with a vengeance. The new hair is darker and more coarse, and sometimes it will even bring a buddy hair along with it.

We must have answers now. But then again, maybe it's better that we don't know. Some mysteries are better left alone.

When solving problems, dig at the roots instead of just hacking at the leaves.
—Anthony J. D'Angelo

14

Bumper Stickers for Middle-Agers

- ✿ I snore, therefore deal with it.
- ✿ Friends don't let friends drive napping.
- ✿ If you can read this, thank your bifocals.
- ✿ Let me repeat myself. And also, let me repeat myself.
- ✿ I ♥ my air-conditioner.
- ✿ Driver carries no money. He can't remember where he left it. He doesn't even know he's driving.
- ✿ The light at the end of the tunnel is your optometrist.
- ✿ Got Supp-Hose?
- ✿ I brake for leg cramps.
- ✿ Honk if you have all your original body parts.

15

Speak Now or Forever Hold Your Peace

The rumors of my death are greatly exaggerated.
—Mark Twain

Nine days after a 6.6 earthquake hit Bam, Iran, rescue workers managed to pull a ninety-seven-year-old woman from the rubble—alive, uninjured, and apparently, quite thirsty. According to reports, the elderly lady credited God with her amazing miracle of survival, then she asked for a cup of tea. When rescue workers brought it to her, she thanked them, then mustered up just enough energy to complain that it was too hot.

Obviously, somewhere along the way to her ninety-seventh birthday, this incredible woman had learned the importance of speaking up. Not only had she survived the massive earthquake, but she had survived ninety-seven years on this earth. She knew that alone entitled her to a few things, and one of them was to have her tea at whatever temperature she so desired. Good for her!

No matter how old you happen to be right now, you, too, have earned the right to speak up. Life gives you that right. Babies know that. They come into the world and immediately they start letting us know what they want.

"Wah!" ("I want my milk!")

"Wah!" ("I want a cookie!")

"Wah!" ("I want those $100 sneakers!")

And so it goes.

Somewhere between birth and middle age, however, some of us forget about the importance of letting our needs (or even our wants) be known. That's not to say that we should act like spoiled children. But if we've allowed the pendulum to swing too far away from our needs because we didn't want to rock the boat, or we've tried our best not to get in anyone's way, maybe it's time to take a lesson from a ninety-seven-year-old woman in Iran and speak up.

It's not easy, though. Especially if you're used to being non-confrontational.

"My foot? Yes, as a matter of fact your car did just roll over it, but don't worry. I'm sure the feeling will return eventually."

"I'm sorry. How thoughtless of me to try to order my food while you are standing in line behind me talking on the cell phone. I hope I didn't disturb your call."

Many of us have been performing the role of doormat for so long, it's become a very comfortable role. What we're forgetting, however, is the simple fact that each of us was made for a reason. We have a purpose. A mission. And to achieve that mission, from time to time we're going to have to speak up. If we constantly allow our voice to be silenced, then our mission will be routed.

A friend of mine used to tell me that when I reached a certain age, I would find it easier to speak up for myself. She said that it was just something that seems to kick in after forty. She was right. Maybe it's because we finally realize in the second half of our lives that our peace of mind is just as important as anyone else's peace of mind. As is our happiness. And as is our truth.

Still, the choice is ours. We can live our lives, or we can let others, circumstances, and fear limit us.

The fact that you're still around today is no accident. Recall the first major illness or accident that you had as a child. If you had lived a hundred years ago, you probably would not have survived it. Medicine has made so many advances over the last hundred years that many of the things that used to take someone's life back then require nothing more than a prescription today.

But you weren't alive back then, you're alive now. And so far you have survived everything that life has brought your way. Clearly, you have a purpose. So speak what's on your heart. Share your ideas, your opinions, and your suggestions for improving the world. Don't let others intimidate you out of standing up for what you believe. Whether you're 44, 64, or 84, you're a survivor. Don't hide away in your house, just watching year after year after year slip by. Do something. Be active. There's a reason that you're still here. Live like it.

We are the hero of our own story.
—Mary McCarthy

16

I Am Not Hungry, I Am Not Hungry, I Am Not Hungry

Never eat more than you can lift.
—Miss Piggy

I'm on the metric diet. It's a great diet plan. You just buy a scale that measures your weight in metric. You can eat whatever you want and never break 100.

Extra weight and middle age just seem to go together, don't they? For whatever reason, we wake up one morning and discover we're retaining more water than Atlantis. We can't fit into most of our clothes, and we figure there is only one thing to do—go on a diet, right?

If you watch television, listen to the radio, read magazines and junk mail, you would get the impression that we are obsessed with dieting. Each year it seems some new fitness guru comes out with a new way for us to lose weight (and for him or her to become a millionaire). There's the no-carb diet, the low-carb diet, the low-fat diet, the high-carb/low-fat diet, the no-sugar diet, the interrogation diet (you don't eat anything, but are still accused of it), and of course, the shame diet (a personal trainer follows you along the buffet line muttering insults under his breath).

"You're not really going to eat that, are you?"

"Fried corn on the cob? Where's that on your diet plan?"

"This is your third plate, you know. I don't care if it is a saucer, it still counts!"

So what's the best diet, the one that will help you lose the most weight and get your personal trainer or other weight-loss cheerleaders off your back?

Good question. No matter how many promises they make, it all comes down to this: the best diet is the one that works best for you. Weight Watchers, Jenny Craig, South Beach, and Atkins all offer plenty of amazing testimonials. But if those diet plans don't work for your body, what good are they to you? We're all different. The perfect diet for you might be the worst diet for me, and vice versa. So we experiment. We try this one and that one and that other one until we finally find a diet plan that will give us the results we want.

But why does losing weight have to be so hard anyway? The answer is simple. Science is once again missing the obvious solution. Science should be working to find a way to put the most calories in the food products that we like the least, and the least calories in the food products that we like the best. If they would figure out a way to do this, our problems would be solved. Imagine the dialogue.

"Brussels sprouts? They look good, but I'd better not. Gotta watch the ol' waistline, you know."

"No cauliflower for you, young man, until you finish all that Cinnabon!"

"You've had enough carrots, sweetie. They're going to ruin your dinner. If you must eat something, eat some brownies."

Now I ask you, doesn't that make a lot more sense? Why should we continue to force ourselves to eat the right foods when all we have to do is make the food we hate the enemy and turn what we love into health food. We need to take the calories out of that banana split and put them into cabbage where they belong. Why should we hold our noses every time we eat broccoli? We all know that broccoli is good for us, but come on, it's a flower.

All we would need to do is take the nutrients and low calorie count of broccoli and switch it with, say, a funnel cake. Who among us would complain about that? Imagine funnel cakes being touted as the latest breakthrough in healthy eating, with dieticians telling us to have at least three servings of it a day. Imagine seeing the heart-friendly symbol next to it on the menu. It brings a tear to your eye, doesn't it?

My sincere hope is that someone reading this book will be moved to dedicate his or her life to this revolutionary dietary research. Perhaps I'm speaking to you, or to one of your children or grandchildren. Whoever it is, if you would do this for your world, you would be doing us all a great service. One of these days we could be hearing about the Sara Lee Diet Plan, the Ben and Jerry's Weight Loss System, and the "Krispy Kreme

10 Days to a Brand-New You" Challenge. You know who you are. I hereby leave it in your hands.

> **The second day of a diet**
> **is always easier than the first.**
> **By the second day, you're off it.**
> —Jackie Gleason

17

The Raven-ing

Once upon a diet dreary,
I lay famished, weak, and weary,
hunger pangs too fast and numerous
for my stomach to ignore.
Bathroom scale, it was just mocking.
Still, I would have eaten caulking,
if somebody wasn't knocking,
knocking at my condo door.
"O be Pizza Hut!" I muttered,
knocking at my condo door.
"Double Cheese, I'm praying for!"
I was on the Atkins Diet
'til a breadstick caused a riot.
On to Weight Watchers to try it,
hoping that I could eat more.
But they had a rule they followed—
a whole ham could not be swallowed.
So in self-pity I wallowed,

licking crumbs up off my floor.
Then I heard more of that knocking,
tapping, rapping at my door,
and wondered who it could be for.
Oh, I've dreamed of eating Twinkies,
licking filling off my pinkies.
Scrambled eggs and sausage linkies.
Little Debbie cakes galore!
Dreamed of sourdough from 'Frisco,
every snack sold by Nabisco,
chocolate bars and even Crisco.
Could I last a second more?
I was starved down to my core!
    Drat this diet evermore!
It is water I'm retaining,
that's the reason for my gaining.
And don't think that I'm complaining,
I just need to eat some more!
I love fat, I won't deny it.
Food is better when you fry it!
See a Snickers and I buy it,
then I keep on wanting more!
    Drat this diet ever more!
So I turned the knob and then I
opened up the door, but when I
saw the one who wanted in, I
had to shut the door again.
'Twas my trainer looking for me,
to work out, she would implore me.
How I wish she'd just ignore me!
But I was late for my weigh-in.

"Look at all the weight you've packed on!
All the burgers you have macked on!
All the Ding Dongs you have snacked on!"
She never screamed like that before.
With the accusations flying,
I assured her I was trying.
I was starving, maybe dying,
But she heard me out no more.
Made me promise I would diet,
then told me to just be quiet.
Exercise? I was to try it,
so I did what she implored.
I stepped back and took position.
I would stop her inquisition.
Did a leg lift in submission,
as I'd kick her out the door!
    Drat this diet evermore!
Now I'm back to eating Twinkies,
licking filling off my pinkies.
scrambled eggs and sausage linkies,
Little Debbie cakes galore.
I don't need no weight loss planning.
Workout tapes I will be banning.
In the space I'll end up spanning,
I'll be happy to my core!
    And I'll be hungry *nevermore*!

18

The Super Senior Bowl

You guys line up alphabetically by height.
—Bill Peterson,
Florida State football coach

If there isn't one already, someone needs to start a seniors' football league.

There's a Senior Tour in golf and it seems to be doing rather well, so why not advance the concept and have one in football? The baby boomer generation would be avid fans. It would be our chance to see all our favorite players who have long since retired.

A few rules of the game would have to be changed, of course.

For one thing, the center wouldn't be required to bend over for the snap. It might take too long for him to get back up, and that clock is ticking. Even the word "snap" might need to be changed since it could cause the team doctor to rush unnecessarily onto the field with a splint.

Instead of assigning arbitrary numbers to all the players, I would suggest they simply put their ages on the jerseys. That way, we could follow the game a little more easily and have a greater understanding of the plays.

"Number 72 hikes the ball to 60 who passes it to number 80. What a throw! He hasn't passed anything like that since that kidney stone in '83. And yes! The pass is good! 80 takes the ball and runs . . . er, walks . . . er, is being carried to the 32-yard line. But not before being tackled by 78 and the rest of the opposing team. Ladies and gentlemen, take a look at that pileup! Have you ever seen anything like that before? All the players are down and a stretcher is being brought onto the field even as we speak. But who's it for? 78? 80? All of them? . . . Wait a minute, wait a minute. It appears . . . yes, yes, someone is already on the stretcher! I don't believe it! The stretcher is carrying the replacement linebacker! Now, that's something you don't see every day, a player being carried onto the field. But number 92 is not just any player, folks. He's the oldest player in Senior Football League history. Who can forget that game when he broke the record for most yardage? One hundred and twelve yards! (Sixty-eight yards to the end zone and 44 more to the rest room!)"

Of course, you can't have a seniors' league without cheerleaders.

"I'm tellin' ya, folks, in all my years of covering professional sports, I've never seen cheerleaders move like that! You'd think those oxygen tanks would slow them down, but these gals are out there giving it everything they've got! And even though that one gal still hasn't gotten up from those splits she did during the first quarter, this is one impressive pep squad! And sure, we all remember that one awkward moment when they threw one of the gals up in the air, and before she came down, they had forgotten what they had done with her. But did they quit? Did they give up? Did they catch her? No! But they didn't let that

stop them. They hung in there and kept on cheering. These gals have spirit! Why, just listen to them cheer.

"2–4–6–8, what disc can we herniate? All of them! All of them! Yea!"

Yes, from the team to the cheerleaders to the traditional pouring of the Geritol over the coach's head, a seniors' football league would be great fun to watch. And I haven't even talked about the wave yet.

"Here it comes."

"Here what comes?"

"The wave. Get ready!"

"Okay, but who am I waving to?"

"Nobody."

"Then why do you want me to wave?"

"It's what you do at football games."

"We're at a football game?"

"Never mind. It's over."

"Who won?"

"Not the game. The wave is over."

"Just as well. I'm not waving at anyone unless you tell me who it is I'm waving to!"

All right, so maybe the concept needs a little work. But I still think it's worth a try. Why, I can hear the vendors now. "Get your granola! Get your soy! Get your prune danish!"

**We're going to turn this team
around 360 degrees.**
—Jason Kidd

19

Classic Tunes Updated for Aging Baby Boomers

- ❀ Hank Williams—"Your Skippin' Heart" (formerly "Your Cheatin' Heart")
- ❀ Glen Campbell—"By the Time I Get My Teeth In" (formerly "By the Time I Get to Phoenix")
- ❀ Otis Redding—"Sittin' at the Doctor's All Day" (formerly "Dock of the Bay")
- ❀ The Platters—"Sweat Gets in My Eyes" (formerly "Smoke Gets in Your Eyes")
- ❀ Paul Anka—"Put Ben-Gay on My Shoulder" (formerly "Put Your Head on My Shoulder")
- ❀ Aretha Franklin—"R-U-N-A-A-R-P?" (formerly "R-E-S-P-E-C-T")

- The Supremes—"Where Did My Mind Go?" (formerly "Where Did Our Love Go?")
- Elvis Presley—"Blue Suede Orthotics" (formerly "Blue Suede Shoes")
- The Tokens—"Can't Get to Sleep Tonight" (formerly "The Lion Sleeps Tonight")
- Elvis Presley—"That's All Right, Grandma" (formerly "That's All Right, Mama")
- Gene Pitney—"It Hurts to Be This Old" (formerly "It Hurts to Be in Love")
- Neil Sedaka—"Standing Up Is Hard to Do" (formerly "Breaking Up Is Hard to Do")
- Bobby Vee—"Take Good Care of My Knee Joints" (formerly "Take Good Care of My Baby")
- Marvin Gaye—"I Heard It Through My Beltone" (formerly "I Heard It Through the Grapevine")
- Perry Como—"Catch a Falling Friend" (formerly "Catch a Falling Star")
- Elvis Presley—"All Hooked Up" (formerly "All Shook Up")
- The Supremes—"You Can't Hurry Me" (formerly "You Can't Hurry Love")
- Ricky Nelson—"There Goes My Figure" (formerly "There Goes My Baby")
- Martha & The Vandellas—"Hot Flash" (formerly "Heat Wave")
- Roy Rogers—"Yellow Toes of Texas" (formerly "Yellow Rose of Texas")
- The Comets—"Nap Around the Clock" (formerly "Rock Around the Clock")

20

High-Fiving Thighs

What you eat standing up doesn't count.
—Beth Barnes

My inner thighs never used to be this close. In all the years that I've been hanging around them, the right one has stayed to the right side of my body, and the left one has stayed to the left. This has been the understanding between them, and they've respected each other's space. They've been cooperative and dutiful. Whenever I walked, one didn't trespass on the other's territory, and they didn't slap each other in some high-fiving thigh way. They simply stayed at their post, content, satisfied, and separate.

Since hitting menopause (and, all right I confess, more than my share of all-you-can-eat buffets and southern "meat and threes"), all that has changed. My thighs have gotten a lot friendlier with each other. They overlap a good two or three inches and whip against each other every time I take a step. It's like I've grown my own mud flaps.

No one really knows about this but me. For the most part, all of this thigh trespassing takes place under my clothing, and most people have no hint that anything out of the ordinary is happening. But it is. Sometimes the friction is enough to heat the wrinkles right out of my jeans. And it can be noisy, too. Sometimes people turn their heads as I walk by and comment,

"Did you hear that?"

"Yeah, what was it?"

"It sounded like two cats fighting on a leather sofa."

Like other changes in middle age, these thigh appendages seem to have appeared with no warning. One day I fit into my jeans perfectly fine, and the next day I'm needing to line them with Vaseline just to get them past my knees. Perhaps this is why so many middle-agers and seniors have insomnia. Considering all the bodily changes that keep happening during the night, we're afraid to go to sleep!

They say Pilates is good for toning and shaping the upper thighs, so I'm seriously thinking about giving it a try (interpreted, that means I've bought the tape but haven't opened it yet).

In the meantime, I guess I have no other choice but to put up with all the fighting my thighs are doing with every step I take.

"Hey, get back over on your own side!"

"Oh, yeah? Who's gonna make me?"

"This is my territory!"

"No, it's not. I was here first!"

"Were not!"

"Were too!"

"Were not!"
It's sad, isn't it? And they used to get along so well.

I don't jog, if I die I want to be sick.
—Abe Lemons

21

Going Through the Changes

Change is inevitable—
except from a vending machine.
—Robert C. Gallagher

They say wisdom comes with age. And in a lot of ways that's true. We've had a lot of time to think about how we can improve the world if only given the chance. They may not all be great ideas, but some could be pure genius. But who asks us? We're walking around with all this wisdom, and no one is coming up to us and inquiring as to how we'd run things. I haven't received any calls from the president, have you? No one from Congress has called either. The governor hasn't even stopped by for a chat and a burger while we discuss the affairs of the state.

The phone company hasn't sent anyone to my house to see if there's any way to improve their service to me. And no one from CBS, NBC, ABC, or FOX has called my house to see if their programming is to my liking. No one's asking me if I have any better ideas about how to run the world. I do, and I'm sure you do, too. But all our input is being forced to stay put. It's their loss, of course.

The first change that I would make would be with the calendar. I've long felt that some months deserve more days while other months could be greatly improved if their allotment was cut back just a little. Take April, for example. The way I see it, April really only needs fifteen days. After tax day, April is basically over. We don't want to think about April anymore. We're ready to put it all behind us and move on to May. Why pretend we're enjoying the second half of April? We're miserable and April knows it. Let's be honest with ourselves and move on.

On the other hand, December is a fun month and should be extended. Especially the period of time between Christmas and New Year's Eve. Who among us couldn't use another week to handle all the gift returns, out-of-town relatives, and the writing of our New Year's resolutions? We would take the days that we took from April and add them all to December.

February is long overdue for some extra days as well. February has been shortchanged for years and I don't think anyone really knows why. What kind of trouble can a month get into anyway? What could February possibly have done to deserve such treatment? February is the "love" month. It's been bringing us warm and fuzzy feelings for a long time now, but how do we repay it? We make it a junior month, a second-stringer, a mini-page on the calendar of life. It gives us romance and we give it inferiority in return. Oh, every four years we feel guilty enough to throw an extra day its way for leap year, but even with that, it only brings February's count up to twenty-nine days, which is still shorter than all the other months. February is not stupid. It

knows what's been going on. February's been a real trooper, and
it's high time we rewarded that kind of dedication to duty. The
new calendar that I propose would be an attempt to make up
for all the years of calendar abuse and grant February another
four weeks. February would go from being the shortest month
to being the longest. It would be a sort of "Take that!" to those
day hogs like January, March, May, and July. Not to mention
August, October, and December. It would finally be February's
time to shine.

June is a month for weddings and could, I'm sure, use a few
more weekends just to accommodate them all. I wouldn't give
June any more workdays, though, because traditionally June is a
vacation month. Who wants more workdays in a vacation month?

As for November, for all intents and purposes, it's over after
Thanksgiving. True, there are all the after-Thanksgiving sales,
but their focus is really Christmas and they rightfully belong in
the month of December.

Another thing that I would change is television. In my opinion, television still skews too young. That's why you'll never see
Geriatric Survivor: Last Senior Standing, or *My Big, Fat, Obnoxious
Retirement Party.* The ironic thing, though, is we're the ones
who are probably watching the most television. My husband
watches the Weather Channel like it's a mini-series.

"Can we turn it now? It's been four days and nothing's changed."
"All right, one more Local on the 8s and I hand over the remote."

He watches the History Channel, Discovery Channel, Ani-
mal Planet, and whatever looks good on the networks and
other cable stations. I watch the twenty-four-hour news programs, *Everybody Loves Raymond* reruns, and some of the new

reality shows. I also watch the Home and Garden Network, and we always try to watch *Meet the Press*. Like teenagers, we flip through the channels with our remote controls, looking for something interesting to watch. With only a hundred stations to choose from, that's not always easy.

We like some of the new season's programs, and we don't care for others. We like some of the made-for-TV movies, and we don't care for others. We like some of the late-night talk shows, and we don't care for others. We have our own tastes, to be sure, but give us quality shows and I think you'd be surprised at how many of us middle-agers would watch them.

Another thing that I would change about the world are all the perfume and cologne samples that advertisers keep putting in magazines. You know the ones I'm talking about, those little inserts where you simply peel back the protective strip and get a whiff of whatever aroma they happen to be advertising. If you have allergies like me, one pass through the magazine can leave you sneezing for hours. So I would like to make a suggestion: Instead of perfume and cologne samples, why don't they give us something we could really use? Scratch-and-taste samples of some of their featured recipes? *Bon Appétit* magazine could really be "bon appétit." You could lick yourself a four-course meal by page 28.

I don't know if any of my suggestions will be taken seriously or not, but that's all right. I am speaking up, and that's the important thing.

> *A fanatic is one who can't change his mind and won't change the subject.*
> —Winston Churchill

22

Suggested Movies for Middle-Agers

* *Hey, Dude, Where's My Teeth?*
* *Legally Gray*
* *Florida's Most Wanted*
* *Gangs of Palm Beach*
* *Cold Feet Manor*
* *Near-Total Recall*
* *Man in the Iron Lung*
* *Sleepless in Every City*
* *Catch You If I Can*
* *The Rock (And the Rest of My Kidney Stones)*

23

When I'm an Old Lady

When our youngest son was an adolescent, my husband had him write a note and sign it, stating that my husband could live in his garage when he was old. My husband grew up living in a one-car garage, so it was one of those, "Just give me a garage and I'll be happy" sort of discussions that led to the note. It was really just a joke, but my husband had it framed and proudly shows it off to guests. I don't have a note yet. I'll have to get one though, because living with my children, getting on their nerves, embarrassing them, and being demanding is the one thing to look forward to in old age. It pays them back for those 2 A.M. feedings, the temper tantrums, the spilled milk, and everything else!

I'm not sure who wrote the following, but it says it all.

When I'm an Old Lady

When I'm an old lady, I'll live with each kid,
And bring so much happiness . . . just as they did.
I want to pay back all the joy they've provided,

Returning each deed. Oh, they'll be so excited!
When I'm an old lady and live with my kids.
I'll write on the walls with reds, whites, and blues,
And bounce on the furniture, wearing my shoes.
I'll drink from the carton and then leave it out.
I'll stuff all the toilets and oh, how they'll shout!
When I'm an old lady and live with my kids.
When they're on the phone and just out of reach,
I'll get into things like sugar and bleach.
Oh, they'll snap their fingers and then shake their head,
And when that is done I'll hide under the bed!
When I'm an old lady and live with my kids.
When they cook dinner and call me to eat,
I'll not eat my green beans or salad or meat.
I'll gag on my okra, spill milk on the table,
And when they get angry I'll run . . . if I'm able!
When I'm an old lady and live with my kids.
I'll sit close to the TV, through the channels I'll click,
I'll cross both eyes just to see if they stick.
I'll take off my socks and throw one away,
And play in the mud 'til the end of the day!
When I'm an old lady and live with my kids.
And later in bed, I'll lay back and sigh;
I'll thank God in prayer and then close my eyes.
My kids will look down with a smile slowly creeping,
And say with a groan, "She's so sweet when she's sleeping!"
When I'm an old lady and live with my kids.

Author Unknown

24

Striking It Rich

I used to sell furniture for a living.
The trouble was, it was my own.
—Les Dawson

If you've made it to middle age, chances are you've seen your share of ups and downs in your financial standing. It doesn't matter if you invested in real estate, the stock market, gold bars, or collectibles, they've all had their share of fluctuations.

When we were newlyweds, my husband and I bought land in the desert. It was our retirement investment. The salesman convinced us to buy the parcel with the tease that it would be worth some hundred thousand dollars in ten years or so.

It's been three decades now and it's not worth much more than what we paid for it, not even counting the interest. The problem is some years ago the government deemed the area a sanctuary for a rare gnat. (I'll wait a moment while you reread that last sentence.) Now that you know there is nothing wrong with your eyes, merely our investment instincts, I'll continue.

Our investment property has become a sort of gnat refugee camp, and so far there's been nothing that we can do about it. We haven't been able to build any permanent structure on the land because it might disturb the natural environment for the gnat. We can sell the property, but we wouldn't get very much for it. Gnats don't carry a lot of cash and humans prefer getting a little more return on their investments. So there it sits, gathering tumbleweeds and fast-food trash, and I assume, more gnats.

That's not the only investment that hasn't panned out for us. We invested in art, too. Our pieces haven't gone up in value as much as we'd like, except for the one on velvet. I think that's because the artist hand-signed it down by Elvis's right leg.

We also used to have some antique crystal and depression glass that my husband had inherited from his mother. The Northridge, California, earthquake took care of any monetary value of those. I salvaged the sentimental value, though, by gathering up some of the pieces to put into a mosaic someday.

And therein lies my point. Nothing is guaranteed for us in life. We can make a fortune in the stock market and lose it all the next week. Real estate can boom and bust, and we can boom and bust right along with it. Collectibles are only worth what someone is willing to pay for them. One year they could command a fortune, the next year we can't give them away.

The true value of a possession, the unchangeable value, will always be the sentimental value. It isn't the house that's worth so much, it's the memories you made in it. It's the Christmases you spent sitting around the fireplace while you watched *It's A Wonderful Life* or *A Christmas Story* on television. It's all those nights the family spent playing board games around the table.

Or the late-night talks you had with your children, sitting on the edge of their beds. No matter what our real-estate appraiser says, it's the memories that determine the real value of a home.

By the same token, the only truly valuable works of art in our possession are the paintings and sculptures created by our children or grandchildren, the ones that are so proudly displayed on our refrigerator doors. They may not be hung in the Getty Museum or in the Metropolitan Museum of Art, but their value is priceless for they are truly irreplaceable.

When we look at our possessions in this way, it won't matter if the value of our home goes up or down, if the stock market soars or plunges, or if our collectibles collect worth or not, for we'll know that we are wealthy in the things that really matter.

**_You cannot have everything.
I mean, where would you put it?_**
—Steven Wright

25

Broadway for Middle-Agers

- ✿ *Annie, Get Your Girdle*
- ✿ *Gramma Mia!*
- ✿ *After the Fall . . . And I Can't Get Up*
- ✿ *I Love You, You're Perfect, Now . . . What Was I Talking About?*
- ✿ *A Raisin in the Mirror*
- ✿ *Beauty and the Plastic Surgeon*
- ✿ *Bunion King*
- ✿ *I'm Miserables*
- ✿ *West Side Bursitis*
- ✿ *Owe Rent*
- ✿ *Much Ado About Cholesterol*
- ✿ *Hello, Doctor!*

26

All Puffed Up

A woman is as old as she looks before breakfast.
—Ed Howe

Middle age has made me puffy. I never used to be puffy. Puffy wasn't a look I was going for, and as far as I know, puffiness has never been featured on the cover of women's magazines as the latest beauty secret. You won't read articles titled "Ten Sure Ways to Puff Up by Summer" or "Where Celebrities Go to Puff." But for some reason, puffiness of varying degrees seems to show up in middle age unannounced, unexpected, and most definitely unwelcomed.

Before I go on, I should clarify one thing. The puffiness that I am referring to is not the same puffiness that I and others like me tend to get after three trips to the buffet counter. Buffet-induced puffiness at least brings with it the memory of fried chicken, potatoes, gravy, and pecan pie to help us cope. Middle-aged puffiness offers no such memories. Its stealth arrival is usually in the middle of the night. The puffee (person doomed to puff) has no idea that it is coming. She simply goes to bed one night looking perfectly normal, and by morning, she's the Michelin Man.

I say "she," but it happens to men, too, and men have the added danger of the necktie. This is of grave concern because the necktie can develop noose-like qualities as the puffage increases. A noose is not a good fashion look.

Aside from the swelling neck area, under-eye swelling is another concern. Often called "bags," these little pockets of puff can make one appear older than he or she actually is. I don't know if it's true, but I read somewhere that applying a dab of Preparation H under each eye is supposed to help. But two words of caution. First, I would check with your doctor before dabbing any medication under your eyes. And second, be careful not to mix up the tube of hemorrhoid cream with your tube of foot cream. Hemorrhoid cream tends to promote shrinkage, and I'm not positive, but this could be why some older people keep getting shorter.

Another part of the body that is prone to puffiness is the cheek area. This seems to be the area where I have my biggest problem. My cheeks have puffed up so much that squirrels have been known to follow me home just to see where I hide my stash of nuts.

My hands can get puffy, too. So much so that even though I know it's there, I haven't seen my wedding ring in over four months.

And if you tend to be as sedentary as I am, your legs can really puff up, especially as the day wears on. I can put on a pair of baggy jeans in the morning, and by mid-afternoon, I need the Jaws of Life to get me free from them. And let me tell you, there's nothing more embarrassing than having to be cut from denim. At least with a real accident, there's an emergency vehicle on stand-by and people are hovering over you, assuring you that everything's going to be all right. But trust me, no one cares about someone getting rescued from a pair of Wranglers.

"Is she going to be all right?"

"It's her own fault. Denim can only stretch so much."

The most serious puffage, however, occurs in the feet and ankles area. Too many of us don't get up and get our blood circulating like we used to. We spend our day either sitting at our computers, behind the steering wheel of our car, at the dinner table, or on the sofa in front of our television sets without so much as a twitch of a toe.

Regular movement is the best way to keep the puff at bay. That, and whenever possible, keep your feet elevated. (This is a little difficult to do while driving, unless you have cruise control. Even so, you might get a ticket if your feet are blocking the windshield.)

Another helpful tip in combating the puff problem is our choice of apparel. For me, turtlenecks are a big no-no. It has been my experience that turtlenecks will merely exaggerate puffiness. I wore a turtleneck for our family portrait last year and my cheeks appeared to block out two family members who were standing behind me. Like my wedding ring, I knew they were there, but no one could see them.

Choice of jewelry is another consideration. Depending on the level of water retention one happens to be experiencing at the moment, choker necklaces can be considered a form of slow suicide. Hence, the name "choker." Longer necklaces are far more flattering and will permit you to continue to indulge in that activity that has become a favorite among so many of us—breathing.

So whether right now you're a pre-puff, mid-puff, or post-puff, just remember it's not your fault. This kind of puffing has nothing to do with eating and everything to do with middle age. No matter how bloated you feel, just know that you are every bit as pretty or handsome as you ever were. And though the event happened years ago, I myself have taken some solace in those immortal words that were overheard at the dedication ceremony of the Hoover Dam.

"She's a beaut, boys, and boy can she hold the water!"

Happiness can exist only in acceptance.
—Denis De Rougamont

27

Reversal of Misfortune

✸ Sometimes I lie awake at night, and I ask, "Where have I gone wrong?" Then a voice says to me, "This is going to take more than one night."
—Charlie Brown

Have you ever considered keeping a journal of all the mistakes you've made in life? If you're like most of us, it would take more than one journal. Maybe four or five. Or perhaps dozens.

What if you kept another journal to document every time someone has hurt you? That could fill up dozens, too. And how about another journal for all the times you were betrayed, the false accusations you had to endure, and every discouraging remark that was ever spoken to you?

After a while, you would have an awful lot of journals filled with an awful lot of negative memories, wouldn't you? But other than getting all that pain off your chest, what good would they really do?

Maybe there's a better use for all that paper. Instead of

writing about every mistake you've ever made, why not write about all the lessons you've learned from those mistakes? Write down how you've grown from your hurts and failures. Write how it felt to be falsely accused of something, or overlooked for a promotion, or kicked when you were down, and how that experience gave you a little more empathy for others who might have suffered the same pain. Now those would make some interesting reading, wouldn't they?

Unfortunately, we cannot prevent life from bringing us to some pretty painful places. They're not our first destination choices by any means, but nevertheless, they're written down on our ticket and sometimes there's not a lot we can do about the itinerary. It's like flying from California to New York and you have to make one or two stopovers along the way—you didn't ask for those stops, that's just how the ticket came.

Life's little side trips can be like that. We may not have asked for them, and we certainly don't have to enjoy them. But they don't have to affect our final destination. We can continue on our journey, perhaps a little wiser, perhaps a little more determined, but not deterred in the least. Whatever memories and lessons we choose to take away from each of our stops is up to us.

The secret to a happy life is not perfection. It is contentment, and contentment isn't something that can be ordered from QVC or bought and sold on eBay. You can't borrow it from your neighbor or send away for it through a catalog. Contentment is something we have to want, work for, and once we get, do everything we can to keep it.

Contentment doesn't mean that everything has, is, or will go smoothly in your life. It simply means that whatever is happening, you're not going to stress over it. You've given the matter to God to handle (he's better qualified to take care of it anyway), and you're free to live at peace.

So quit dwelling on whatever negatives have come your way. No one has done this thing called "life" without running into a little turbulence along the way. Life is about lessons learned, judgments improved, forgiveness rendered, trust renewed, hurts healed, behaviors changed, boundaries defined, and successes enjoyed even after multiple failures.

Why do you think people say such nice things at funerals? Because their loved ones had no flaws? Hardly. We all have flaws. Individuals are admired at the end of their life not because of their perfection, but because of their perseverance. They may have endured plenty of setbacks, failures, and hurts, but with them came plenty of opportunities for them to shine. And to be content.

> *Many people die at twenty-five and aren't buried until they are seventy-five.*
> —Max Frisch

28

The Rise and Fall of Cellulite

*Laziness is nothing more than
the habit of resting before you get tired.*
—Jules Renard

My husband's uncle, Rev. Anthony dePompa, who is in his nineties, has been doing water aerobics every week for years. Water aerobics are good because they allow you to exercise with less risk of injury. I think I'm going to sign up. I figure that even if I don't get into shape, staying in the water that long would at least give me an excuse for my wrinkles.

There are other reasons why I like the idea of exercising in water. I can blame my extra weight on the optical distortion of the water. I can splash water on my back and shoulders and make it look like I've been sweating. And a pool has got to smell a whole lot better than a gym!

If I never get around to joining a water aerobics class, however, I'm fairly certain I'm still getting a good workout just going about my daily routine. If I had a pedometer, I would know how many miles I walk in a twenty-four-hour period. It has got to be pretty impressive. From the moment I get up in the morning, I'm burning the calories. It's like I'm on my own personal marathon. I walk from the bed to the kitchen to make a couple of Eggos, then walk over to the computer desk to do a single knee bend into my chair, then I do an hour or so of finger exercises on my keyboard before walking to the pantry for a snack.

After that, it's off to the mailbox to check on the mail, then to the refrigerator for a sandwich, and back to the computer for another knee bend and more finger exercises. Then I walk back to the cupboard for a bag of Fritos, giving my arm muscles a good workout just trying to open it. After walking around the family room looking for the remote, I do another knee bend onto the sofa and more finger exercises changing the channels. After another hour or so, I do a sit-up, then get on my feet again and walk to the freezer for some weightlifting (a pint of Ben and Jerry's in each hand), then walk back to the computer for more finger exercises between the keyboard and lifting spoonfuls of Chunky Monkey and Chocolate Chip Cookie Dough to my mouth. Then it's back to the pantry for some chips, and . . . Whew. I'm exhausted just thinking about it!

As you can see, even if I never get around to joining an aerobics class, I think I'm still covered. Besides, I also try to fit in my agitator workout every day. It's my own workout plan that I'm seriously thinking about marketing. The agitator workout is where I sit on my washing machine during the spin cycle and just let it shake the weight off of me. It works a little like the old vibrating belts, only you don't have to stand. The seat's not all that comfortable, but it's a good workout. And whenever it gets an uneven load, I can really feel the burn (especially if I'm using the "Hot-Warm" cycle).

Speaking of vibrating belts, I know I already told the story of my vibrating belt experience in my book *Didn't My Skin Used to Fit?*, so I won't repeat myself here. But suffice it to say that in my own opinion, my new agitator workout is much safer. So be watching for my new workout video to be released.

(All right, I confess. The above tease was just a shameless plug for my other book, so I will go ahead and share the story here, too. It merits being repeated anyway.)

You see, it was like this. I had some cellulite in my arms and legs and wasn't too thrilled about it. I had heard that a vibrating belt might help, so one day I decided to give it a try. I vibrated my legs, hips, and arms, envisioning all the cellulite being shaken from my body and my memory. It felt great.

When I was done, the cellulite of course was still there, but I figured it was just a matter of time before it would all begin to smooth out and I could return to my BC self (before cellulite).

It turned out to be just a matter of *one* night. When I got up that next morning and looked at myself in the mirror, I could not find any upper-arm cellulite. I could not find any upper-arm cellulite because *all of my upper-arm fat had somehow slid down to my elbows!* There were two huge cavities in each of my arms, and my elbows were bulging like Popeye's! I wanted to cry. I wanted to laugh.

I wanted to cry and laugh. I couldn't believe the image staring back at me in the mirror. The ironic thing was I had done it all to myself in an effort to *improve* my body. It was akin to choking to death on a vitamin, or perhaps drowning while attempting a push-up in a water aerobics class.

I made an appointment with my doctor who examined me, then called a partner of his into the office to take a look.

"How'd you say you did this again?" he asked.

I told him, and they both just stared at me in amazement. There wasn't anything they could do. So I quit wearing short sleeves and tried my best to hide my Popeye arms.

I thought I was going to have to live like that for the rest of my life, but after two years I awoke one morning, glanced at myself in the mirror, and noticed something interesting. My upper-arm fat that had slid down to my elbows had somehow made the return trip. Just as mysteriously as it had fallen, it had risen to duty once again, as though nothing had ever happened.

Now, granted, this was just *my* experience. You could try a vibrating belt and have perfectly fine results. But I think I'm going to stick with my agitator workout program. The only danger I see with that is falling off the machine. And if that happens, there is usually a full basket of laundry nearby that I can aim for.

> *We all get heavier as we get older because there's a lot more information in our heads.*
> —Vlade Divac,
> NBA basketball player

29

Until

You are as young as your faith,
as old as your doubt,
as young as your self-confidence,
as old as your fear,
as young as your hope,
as old as your despair.
—Paul H. Duhn

Now that we've entered into the second half of our lives, what advice do we have for others on the best way to cope? Attitude.

It's all about attitude.

- ✿ Be positive *until* your circumstances improve.
- ✿ Be generous *until* you aren't even aware of your sacrifices.
- ✿ Be curious *until* there is nothing left to learn.
- ✿ Be unconditionally loving *until* you no longer need to be loved unconditionally.
- ✿ Be courageous *until* there is nothing left to stand up for.

✿ Be content *until* you need nothing more than what you already have.

✿ Be available *until* you hardly notice the inconvenience.

✿ Be joyful *until* the sadness is healed.

✿ Be forgiving *until* you need no forgiveness from anyone, anywhere, anytime.

✿ Be thankful *until* you run out of things to be thankful for.

A positive attitude may not solve all your problems, but it will annoy enough people to make it worth the effort.

—Herm Albright

30

Picture This

*Beauty is in the eye of the beholder; but it may
be necessary, from time to time, to give a stupid,
or misinformed beholder, a black eye.*
—Miss Piggy

Pictures. One snap of the camera and they've captured a
moment, a memory, and sometimes every wrinkle and dark circle on our faces. There are, of course, lighting and makeup
tricks that can help, as well as special lenses that a photographer can use. But everyday folks don't always know about
these. Movie stars do. That's why you'll often see magazine
covers featuring a sixty-year-old legend who barely looks forty.
It's not so much a matter of her ageless beauty being captured
on film as it's a matter of a very creative makeup artist and photographer.

The worst pictures for me are the outdoor shots. Have you
ever had someone snap a close-up of you while you're squint-
ing into full sunlight? Your face can end up looking like a page

out of a Rand McNally map. Downtown Cincinnati, to be exact. Every street, or rather, every line and wrinkle shows up. Even the cul-de-sacs.

Some of the best pictures I've seen of others have been taken at glamour photo studios. Have you been to one of these places? Before posing for your photographs, the staff gives you a complete makeover. They do your hair and makeup, then let you select an outfit from their collection of glamour clothing, or if you'd prefer you can bring your own change of clothes.

One year, I took my mother to have glamour photos taken and we surprised the family with the photographs at Christmas. My mother was a beautiful woman, even without any makeup. But after the professional makeover, she looked amazing. Which brings up another point. If AARP doesn't already sponsor one, I think they should sponsor a beauty contest for middle-agers and above. There certainly wouldn't be any shortage of contestants. Sophia Loren, Diane Keaton, Connie Stevens, Meryl Streep, Oprah Winfrey. Do any of these celebrities look like little old ladies to you? And that's not even counting all the non-celebrities who could compete.

So let the snapping begin. Make your appointment with that professional photographer. Book an afternoon at a glamour studio. Or take your own. Say cheese and start capturing those Kodak moments of your life. Pictures are how you and your family and friends get to relive their favorite times with you. Pictures capture birthdays, vacations, reunions, parties, graduations, family weddings, and every other event of your life. They're your mind's memories preserved forever on photo paper.

Then, once you have them, don't just pack them in a box and hide them away in the attic or closet, never to be enjoyed again. Take them out and show them off. Pass on their stories to the next generation. Relive those moments. That's what pictures are all about. They're history. Your history. They let future generations know you were here. And they remind everyone just how beautiful you are . . . No matter how many birthdays you've celebrated.

As a white candle
In a holy place,
So is the beauty
Of an aged face.
—Joseph Campbell

31

Geritol Gangsters

I had to stop driving my car for a while . . .
the tires got dizzy.
—Steven Wright

I once got a ticket for going 35 miles per hour in a 25-mile-per-hour zone. What can I say? I'm a rebel.

But that's the kind of tickets we middle-agers get. You won't see us standing before a judge trying to explain why we were drag racing down Main Street or why we crammed ten people into a Volkswagen and drove to a rock concert on Friday night. First of all, we prefer matinees, and our idea of racing is beating everyone else to the bread station at the cafeteria.

The kind of driving infractions we commit aren't the kind that get a lot of coverage on *Cops*. We get nabbed for double parking at the walk-in medical clinic. We get written up for jay-walking in front of Wal-Mart. And yes, we get ticketed for going 35 miles per hour in a 25-mile-per-hour zone.

No matter how baggy our pants might be, it's plain to see

that we are not a very tough bunch. We don't look tough, we don't act tough, and we certainly don't talk tough.

"Yo, Earl."

"Whazup, doggie?"

"I think it's supposed to be 'dawg.'"

"Dawg?"

"Yeah. It's 'Whazup, Dawg?'"

"Sorry, housey. My boo boo."

"You mean, 'Sorry, homey. My bad.'"

"Right on. So, what's the haps, Paps?"

"I'm just kickin' it."

"Leg spasms again?"

"Yeah, but I'm just chillin'."

"Circulation problems?"

"Word."

"I hear ya, doggie."

"Dawg."

"Whatever."

Not exactly "gangsta rap," is it? But most of us accept the fact that we're not that hip anymore. Lingo, styles, music, rules, everything keeps changing so fast, we couldn't keep up with all the trends anyway. What's in today is old school tomorrow. Then just wait a decade or two, and it'll start all over again.

There's something to be said for old school, though. Old-school comedy means comedy you can enjoy and not feel embarrassed about. Old-school prices means gasoline you don't need to take out a second mortgage on your home just to purchase. Old-school politics means qualified people running for office without feeding the public's insatiable thirst for scandal, and old-school home prices mean $100,000 will buy more than a park bench.

No, our generation may not be considered cool anymore. We may not say "dawg" or "my bad" or any other hip expressions (or whatever was hip as of this printing). You may not spot us speeding down the freeway in the fast lane. More often than not, we'll be ones in the slow lane just driving along, enjoying the scenery (we use less of that overpriced gasoline that way). We'll be voting for the man or woman we think is best qualified to run the country, no matter how much the media bashes him or her. We'll be supporting entertainment we think is worthwhile, and we'll be staying home more often than most in order to enjoy the house we've been making a lifetime of payments on. And most importantly, we'll be doing it all while wearing comfortable shoes.

All things considered, maybe we are the "cool" ones after all.

The best part of aging in this business is losing that obsession about work and being able to spend a little more time with family.
—Clint Eastwood

32

Laugh Lines

One of the major problems in the world today is that we've lost our sense of humor.
—Leo Buscaglia

You won't see their faces on the walls of post offices around the country. Their profiles won't be featured on *America's Most Wanted*. You won't even read an exposé about them in your town newspaper. But they're threatening our way of life, and somebody needs to stop them.

Who are they? People with no sense of humor.

They're not in the majority, thank goodness, but there are enough of them around to make the rest of us feel more than a little uncomfortable.

These humorless people are easy to spot. They're the ones sitting at that Jerry Seinfeld show, arms crossed, daring him to make them laugh. They're hanging out at Blockbuster or Holly-wood Video, badmouthing all the comedies.

"I hated that movie. Don't rent it. I didn't laugh once."

They may go by different aliases—"Grouch," "Grumpy," "Ol' Stick in the Mud," "Wet Blanket"—but we know who they are and they have one mission in life—to bring the rest of us down.

Laughter is healthy. It has the power to make you forget your problems, even if only temporarily. A hearty laugh can even burn thirty-five calories! How's that for a diet plan? Do without white bread if you want; I'd rather laugh.

Personally, I love to laugh. It's one of my favorite emotions. I'd much rather be in the company of people who love to laugh than people who love to complain.

There are different humor tastes, of course. Some of us like comedy that's a little more sophisticated; others enjoy slapstick. Some like blue-collar humor and jokes about everyday family life; others prefer topical material about what's happening in the news, like the comedy of Jay Leno or David Letterman. Some like physical comedy; others like to hear funny stories, such as the ones told by Bill Cosby and Garrison Keillor. There are those of us who like to get our daily dose of funny by reading the comics in our daily newspaper, while the rest of us prefer getting our daily laughs from our co-workers, friends, and family.

But even with all that laughter going on around us, there are still some folks who just don't get it. They think life is far too serious to laugh about. For whatever reason, they refuse to give themselves permission to laugh.

"I'm too dignified."

"I'm too tired."

"I'm too stressed."

"I'm too old."

So many excuses, so little joy.

But Ward Cleaver was right when he said, "You're never too old to do goofy stuff." A good sense of humor isn't something we outgrow. From the very beginning of our journey to the final chapter, laughter is a necessary part of life. It's like breathing. We have to do it to survive.

So be on the lookout for the humorless. You'll recognize them by the clouds over their heads and the scowls on their faces. Don't let their negative attitudes and sour comments spoil your own zest for life. Protect your joy at all costs.

You can, of course, try reminding these people of the health benefits of laughter and how a cheerful face can take a good ten years off their appearance and even help with their diet plan. But I'd use caution before sneaking up behind them and tickling them, unless you can run really, really fast.

Does God have a sense of humor?
He must have if He created us.
—Jackie Gleason

33

Ten Commandments for Aging

- ✿ Thou shalt not raise up thy pants unto the uttermost parts of thy armpits.
- ✿ Thou shalt not look at thy face in a magnifying mirror, for thy heart's sake.
- ✿ Thou shalt not curse the name of thy dietary plan.
- ✿ Remember the place where thou hast left thy car keys, glasses, and other possessions, or buy tracking devices.
- ✿ Honor the rules of spandex that the circulation in thy legs may be long on this earth.
- ✿ Thou shalt not steal the age of thy neighbor.
- ✿ Thou shalt not commit to baby-sit more than six grandchildren under the age of three at one time, lest thou become a babbling loon.
- ✿ Thou shalt wear comfortable shoes so that thou wouldst not have a harvest of bunions and corns.
- ✿ Thou shalt not bear false witness with thy comb over.

✿ Thou shalt not covet thy neighbor's taco, or hot and spicy sausage, or any other food items that thou knowest will war against the innermost regions of thy body.

34

Will Work for Respect

*If you don't want to work, you have to work
to earn enough money so that
you won't have to work.*
—Ogden Nash

In some industries, there appears to be a prejudice against hiring middle-agers. Employers seem to want to hire only those who have an entire career life to give to the company.

But in today's ever-changing, fast-paced, 401(k)-transferring world, workers don't necessarily have the company loyalty they once did. If another, better offer comes along, they're gone. So career-building arguments no longer seem valid.

Middle-agers, on the other hand, have a lot to offer corporate and industrial America. Instead of easing them out of the work force, employers should be trying to hire as many of them as possible. They have experience, they have knowledge, and they have discipline. But because they also might have gray hair, wrinkles, and a pre–1960 birthday, they're all too often shut out of the employment process.

But for all you potential employers out there, here are just a few advantages awaiting you when you hire someone over forty.

Advantages to Hiring Middle-Agers

- ❀ We won't address you as "Yo, bossman."
- ❀ We won't leave skateboard marks on the walls of the building.
- ❀ We won't call in sick because our new tattoo is infected.
- ❀ You can send us to Milwaukee for a training conference, and we can find it on the map.
- ❀ We're old enough to know that we don't know everything.
- ❀ We'll show more respect for a boss thirty years our junior than some employees show to a boss thirty years their senior.
- ❀ At staff meetings, we'll say "Yes, sir" or "Yes, ma'am," instead of "I'm down with that."
- ❀ We won't use the company phone to call Australia just because we think the accent's cool.
- ❀ We won't argue with you over whether or not we should remove our tongue ring, eyebrow ring, and various other body-piercing jewelry. Outside of the staples from our gall bladder surgery, we're not into having metal accessories stuck in our skin.
- ❀ We would never say to a customer on the phone, "I woke up from my nap for this?"

Opportunity is missed by most people because it comes dressed in overalls and looks like work.
—Thomas Edison

35

The Comb-Over Conspiracy

The most expensive haircut I ever had cost ten pounds. And nine went on the search fee.
—William Hague, England

They're just wrong. I don't believe God ever intended for man to grow his hair as long as possible on one side of his head just to flip it over and wrap it around the other side. This was not in the original design. There is no scripture in Genesis that says, "And God fashioned Adam's comb over and saw that it was good." The comb over is something that man came up with all on his own. Sort of like the Edsel.

But man was wrong.

Now, before I go on, if you are reading this and you happen to have a comb over, you need to know that it is not your fault. Society has told you that it's okay to play this little hair trick on the public. It has told you that no one will notice that your bangs are merely your back hair being combed forward. But society has been leading you on.

Don't get me wrong. You have a right to grow and comb your hair in whatever direction you care to. All I'm saying is don't be disillusioned into thinking that the public isn't aware. We've seen enough bad comb overs to be quite skilled in following a hair to its root, regardless of how far away that root might be.

I've often wondered who came up with the comb-over concept in the first place. Did this person walk in from a windstorm with his hair blown in a dozen different directions, look at himself in the mirror, and say, "It's a miracle! My bald spot's gone!"?

Even with its drawbacks, though, the comb over seems to have a few advantages over the toupee. I knew a man who bought a top-of-the-line toupee and wore it everywhere he went—to the beach, in the shower, golfing. He even played baseball in it. It looked so good, you wouldn't have known he was wearing one had it not been for that one game when he slid into second base and his toupee went on to third. (The incident gave a new meaning to letting the wind blow through your hair. It also made it difficult to score the game because he was called out on second base, but his hair was clearly safe on third.)

As real as they can look, toupees can still fly off, slip off, or slide off when you least expect them to. You can even accidentally put one on backward, like one friend hurriedly did when I surprised him with a hospital visit. I kept telling him to turn around and face me, but then realized he already was.

Hair transplants are another alternative to the comb over. This is where the doctor will take hair from another part of your body and surgically implant it on the top of your head. Some transplants look amazingly natural, while others can leave you looking as if you have little electrodes coming out of your scalp.

Maybe our forefathers had the right idea. George Washington, Thomas Jefferson, and Benjamin Franklin all knew perfectly well how to handle their hair-loss problems: they just threw on a powdered wig.

So maybe that's another good option. Of course, a powdered wig would make some heads turn at the golf course. But considering the shade they'd offer, and the padded protection against stray balls, they might not be such a bad idea.

I love bald men. Just because you've lost your fuzz don't mean you ain't a peach.
—Dolly Parton

36

Pistol-Packing Gramma

On my first day in New York a guy asked me if I knew where Central Park was. When I told him I didn't he said, "Do you mind if I mug you here?"
—Paul Merton

According to reports, the number of seniors buying guns has doubled in recent years. I had no idea that bran had such a serious side effect.

All right, so maybe it isn't the bran. Maybe it's just the times in which we live. It seems every night our news is filled with stories of sniper shootings, carjackings, muggings, and other violent crimes. Seniors, like many of us, might not be feeling all that safe anymore. So a certain percentage of them are beginning to pack heat.

Now, before you start choosing sides on this issue, know this—this chapter isn't a debate over whether or not everyday citizens should have guns. It's merely an observation of the fact that some older members of our society are beginning to feel the need to fight back.

I recall a newspaper report some years ago of a grandmother who purse-whipped a would-be mugger until he finally took off running. No doubt there are plenty of other cases on the police files where an older person has stood up to an assailant. I'm sure the police would say doing that isn't a very good idea in most situations, but apparently some simply reached a point where enough was enough.

Part of the problem is the growing attitude that it's every man for himself. Certainly, we have the Good Samaritan laws for life-threatening emergencies, but people are still hesitant to get involved in other people's problems these days.

I stood in the middle of a very busy street one night in Southern California with a stalled car, and not one person stopped to help me push it out of the way. They sent their encouragement by way of their car horns (and a few other gestures) as they drove past. I had caused a major traffic jam and was prolonging their drive home. My problem had become their problem and they were none too happy about it.

But no one offered to help.

I finally had to leave my car, walk to a gas station, and call home. Two of my sons arrived a short time later and pushed the car out of the street. By then, the traffic jam stretched for miles. I was tired, frustrated, and cold. But I was finally out of everyone's way.

In days gone by, there wasn't a need for the Good Samaritan law. People just instinctively helped.

But these are different times. Today good deeds are sometimes punished. The world is a dangerous place, and helping out a perfect stranger or in some cases, even an acquaintance, can be pretty risky. So maybe it's not so surprising that more and more of the older generation have begun to arm themselves. Again, I'm not saying whether or not I think this is wise. I'm just saying that for whatever reason, it's happening.

Middle-agers, on the other hand, don't seem to be getting caught up in this trend as much as seniors. I don't know if this means they're anti-gun or if it's just because in menopause, packing more heat is definitely not something you want to do.

> **We live in an age when pizza gets to your home before the police.**
> —Jeff Marder

37

Pleasin' the World

I don't know the key to success, but the key to failure is to try to please everyone.
—Bill Cosby

If you've learned anything by the time you reach middle age, chances are you've learned this—you can't please everyone.

Mail carriers have certainly learned this.

"The mail's late again. Can't he ever get it here on time?"

"Did he have to bring me all these bills? Couldn't he have just skipped my house today?"

Police officers know it, too.

"Officer, come quick! There's someone trying to break in my house!"

"Doesn't that cop have anything better to do than to give me a ticket?"

And pastors have also learned it.

"Your preaching's too long."

"Your preaching's too short."

"You never visit."

"You're too intrusive."

No matter what you do, no matter how sincere your motive, somebody isn't going to be happy. Teachers know it. Parents know it. Counselors know it. Interior decorators know it. Hair stylists know it. Politicians know it. Artists know it. And just about everyone else knows it. You can't please everybody.

But we sure try, don't we?

"You can't see the movie over my head? I'm sorry. I'll lie down here on the floor. Is that better?"

"Did I mind waiting for twenty minutes while you answered your other call? Of course not. Maybe you can do a load of laundry, too, while I hold."

The older we get, the more we come to realize that no matter how much of a people pleaser we happen to be, some people have made up their mind not to be pleased. If they are looking to find something to criticize us for, they will most assuredly find it. But by the same token, if they want to find something worth complimenting and encouraging us about, they can find that, too. It just depends on what they're looking for.

So what do you do? Change yourself to accomodate everyone else's tastes, standards, and desires? You be yourself. Not anyone else, just you, the man or woman you were created to be. Certainly, you'll want to strive to be the best you that you can be. But never let anyone's negative comments determine your identity. You are you. No one else can fill that role. And no one else but you has been given the part.

It's sad that it takes so many of us half a lifetime to figure out that being who we are is a pretty good person to be.

When I give a lecture, I accept that people look at their watches, but what I do not tolerate is when they look at it and raise it to their ear to find out if it stopped.
—Marcel Achard

38

Excuse Us

❀ Excuse us if we drive too slowly in front of you. We're taking our time and enjoying the scenery. Have you looked at it lately?

❀ Excuse us if we offer our help when you don't need it. It's not because we think you can't do something, it's because we'd like to see if we still can.

❀ Excuse us if we talk too much about our ailments. We'd love to talk about other things, but no one asks us those questions anymore.

❀ Excuse us if we don't walk fast enough in front of you at airports, malls, and grocery stores. In our heads we are running (and we're leaving you in our dust).

❀ Excuse us if we prefer to watch old movies and comedies. We're from a generation where the good guys won and the comedy wasn't blue. And we liked it better that way.

❀ Excuse us if we want to be spoken to with respect. We were taught to respect our elders, and we have been looking forward to finally being treated that way ourselves. It's been a long time coming. So do us a favor and let us enjoy it.

✿ Excuse us if we ask you to call a little more often. Hearing your voice, even for only a minute, makes our day.

✿ Excuse us if we don't understand body piercing. We're not out of it. We just get enough piercing from our weekly B–12 shots or insulin injections and can't understand why anyone would want to voluntarily get stuck with needles.

✿ Excuse us if it takes us a little extra time to rise from a sitting position. If our knees are weak, it's from a lifetime of hard work. In our day, we admired that in a person.

✿ Excuse us if we forget to wipe our mouths. There's a good chance someone wiped yours plenty of times when you were little.

✿ Excuse us if when you visit, we don't seem to want to let you go. We know we'll have to, we just like to stretch out the moment as long as possible.

✿ Excuse us if we ask for a hug. It reminds us how much we're loved and that's better than the newest miracle drug on the market.

39

First Impressions

I don't plan to grow old gracefully. I plan to have face-lifts until my ears meet.
—Rita Rudner

Have you ever crawled out of bed in the morning, looked in a mirror, and wondered how someone managed to transplant your knee skin to your cheeks during the night without waking you up? Okay, it's not really your knee skin, but for some unknown reason I can wake up in the morning and my face will have taken on every fold, crease, and pucker of my bedding. I can't tell you how many times I have awakened with the impression of a crocheted pillowcase pressed deep into my cheeks. And I don't even own a crocheted pillowcase.

Part of the blame for this lies with the loss of elasticity in our skin over the years. When we were young, a relative could pinch our cheeks and, even though we might not have enjoyed it, the little piles of flesh would return to their natural position within seconds, no harm done. But pinch a middle-aged cheek and it's a different matter altogether. When pinched, middle-aged skin can stay all bunched up, looking not unlike a relief map of the Appalachian Mountain ridge.

Lack of moisture also plays a significant role. Many of us middle-agers suffer from dry skin. Not just regular parched skin. Sahara desert kind of dry, parched skin. The kind of skin that needs its moisturizer spray gunned on. Drinking eight glasses of liquid a day is supposed to help hydrate the skin, as is a good skin moisturizing system. This is especially important if you want to avoid those embarrassing situations like diving into a swimming pool and soaking up all the water like a giant sponge.

In addition to a regular hydration regimen, plenty of products and procedures available today promise to help. There are antioxidant creams, exfoliation processes, and of course, face food. Face food is simply what it says, food for the face. Instead of going into the mouth, these food products are made to go directly on your face. There are lemon and orange masques, peach and mango facial creams, mint and avocado peels, cucumber eye patches, and cherry and peppermint lotions. They're supposed to be good for your skin, but I'm not sure I agree with the whole concept. If I have to be on a diet, why should my face be eating better than I am? Why should I deny my body a slice of pie at Marie Callender's while my face is eating a mango peel?

I do want to take care of my skin, though, so I suppose I'll need to do something. God may be the lifter of our head, but when it comes to our facial skin we're on our own.

I'm so old they've cancelled my blood type.
—Bob Hope

40

Dream a Little Dream

*A man is not old until regrets
take the place of dreams.*
—John Barrymore

We cannot possibly get to this point of our lives without having fulfilled a few dreams, forgotten about some, and still be hanging on to a few others.

Perhaps in our youth we had aspirations of becoming a rock star. But now, the only rock we talk about is the one they removed from our gall bladder. Maybe we dreamed of becoming a Wall Street broker, but never made it out of our hometown, much less all the way to New York.

So what happened? How did we get off track?

The answer is simple—life.

Funny how life has a way of forcing us to reassess our dreams, adjust our sails, and chart out new courses. Perhaps that business degree we were working toward had to be postponed because we lost our job and were forced to drop out of college. Or that art school scholarship had to be forfeited because we needed a job to help support our aging father. Our dreams may have been to become a police officer, an attorney, a minister, or any number of other career choices. But we had to abandon them. Perhaps we made the right decision for the wrong reasons, the wrong decision for the right reasons, or maybe it was apathy that snuffed out our dreams. Or it could be that we were too afraid of the risk and played it safe.

God has designed a life plan for each one of us. It was custom-fitted to our talents and personality, and it usually involves a step of faith. But that step, the first one, is always up to us, because along with his plan, he has also given us the freedom of choice. We can decide to pursue our dreams and be satisfied in the attempt, or we can simply exist, accepting life as it comes and never quite live up to our potential. We can pursue the best, or we can settle for less. It's our decision.

If you've done the latter, if you've settled, the good news is, it's not too late. There are plenty of middle-aged and senior adults who did some of their greatest work and made their biggest impact on society during the second half of their lives— Mother Teresa, Grandma Moses, Colonel Sanders, Ronald Reagan, Winston Churchill, Franklin D. Roosevelt, just to name a few. As Yogi Berra said, "It ain't over 'til it's over."

There is nothing sadder than an unfulfilled life. Someone who is well past the halfway point of life, convinced that they missed out on their true calling. Dreams don't come with expiration dates. Take advantage of the years that lie ahead of you and do what you were created to do, whatever that happens to be. Whether it's in education, politics, science, medicine, arts, or any other field, the world needs what you still have to offer.

I was sixty-six years old. I still had to make a living. I looked at my social security check of $105 and decided to use that to try to franchise my chicken recipe. Folks had always liked my chicken.
—Colonel Harland Sanders

Ten Things I Knew I Would Never Forget Even in Middle Age

1.
2.
3.
4.
5.
6.
7.
8.
9.
10.

(Okay. Never mind.)

For He Was a Jolly Good Fellow

I arise in the morning torn between a desire to improve the world and a desire to enjoy the world. This makes it hard to plan the day.
—E. B. White

One of the cleverest comedy sketches I ever saw was on the old *Tonight Show* with Johnny Carson. Johnny was delivering a eulogy for the creator of the thesaurus. Instead of saying just one word to describe the different aspects of the funeral or the deceased, he went through a long list of synonyms. *"He's away, no longer here, gone to a better place, departed, checked out, belly up, pushing up daisies, kicked the bucket . . ."*

That's not the dialogue verbatim, but you get the picture. It was a very funny idea for a sketch.

Real funeral tributes, however, are usually far from funny. Sometimes they're far from truthful, too.

"He was the most wonderful man I ever knew. He was like a brother to me."

In reality, the deceased hadn't heard from the speaker in over twenty years.

"I don't know what I'm going to do without her. She was my life."

The truth is, when she was alive, the speaker never had a kind word to say about her.

Eulogies, no matter how glowing and eloquent, don't do much good if they're full of sentiments the departed never knew during life. How much better it would be if the speech we write out for someone's funeral were words we had already spoken to him while he was alive.

Life gets hectic. We need to go here, we need to be there, we have to start this, we have to finish that. Deadlines are hovering over our heads, faxes are coming in, cell phones are going off, and computer screens are freezing up on us. We're stressed, overcommitted, booked up, stretched out, and tired. How in the world do we fit in personal relationships? There simply is no time.

Or is there?

Somehow we seem to find the time and the way to rearrange our calendars, put our business matters on hold, and practically move heaven and earth to be there for a loved one's memorial service.

Maybe we could try just a little harder to rearrange our calendars for a luncheon with our friends, or a day in the park with our spouse, or that visit to our children or, in some cases, grandchildren.

None of us knows how much time we have left. We can hope it'll be another fifty years. But there are no guarantees for any of us. As much as we don't like to think about it, we're all going to have to face the end of the party someday. As a comedy writer, I've often wondered if I'll go in some bizarre way. Perhaps my husband will have to tell our friends and loved ones,

"We told her not to use the computer while in the bathtub, but she just mumbled something about a deadline, plugged it in, and deleted herself. We tried to save her as a text file, but we got there too late."

However it happens, or whenever it happens, is not up to us. The only thing we do have power over is to make sure we are making a difference in someone's life each and every day.

Maybe not everyone's life. That would be impossible. But someone's life. And the best place to start is with those who mean the most to us.

They say such nice things about people at their funerals that it makes me sad that I'm going to miss mine by just a few days.
—Garrison Keillor

43

I Hear Ya

You have to endure what you can't change.
—Marie de France

Does anyone know what it is about earlobes that makes them start to sag after middle age? Even people who have never worn earrings find their lobes suddenly hanging a little closer to their shoulders. I myself have had to quit wearing shoulder pads for this very reason. My earlobes kept rubbing against the pads, and I was afraid the friction might cause the foam in them to spontaneously combust.

As far as I know, there is nothing we can do about this ear-lobe problem short of surgery. We can't go on an earlobe diet, and to my knowledge, there aren't any earlobe workout videos on the market.

The size of the actual ear seems to change over the years, too. For reasons unbeknownst to most middle-agers, ears seem to go on a sudden growth spurt after passing age fifty, in some cases growing to incredible proportions. Not large enough

COOKING WITH HOT FLASHES

where involuntary flight was involved, but enough for the average person to note the difference.

Big earlobes don't seem to be as big a problem for women. We can double pierce our ears and fold the lobe upward, pinning back some of the spare flesh. It doesn't look that great, but at least it gets the lobe up off the shoulder pad, reducing the potential for fire.

But what can men do? Other than growing sideburns and a full beard to hide them, or wearing a turtleneck and tucking their lobes under the collar, they don't have much of a choice.

In addition to the fire hazard, elongated lobes can be dangerous in other ways, too. In windstorms, they can get to flapping too much in the crosscurrent and before you know it, you've slapped yourself unconscious. And women need to use caution with curling irons. Some have been known to accidentally curl their lobes with their hair, and aside from the third-degree burns, earlobes really don't look that great in a flip.

So if you've been watching your earlobes growing bigger and bigger year after year, try following the above precautions. They just might save your life. And if you really hate your earlobes, just think about all the shade they provide in the summer.

Know what's weird? Day by day, nothing seems to change, but pretty soon . . . everything's different.
—Calvin from *Calvin and Hobbes*

44

Outgrowing Fun

When I was born I was so surprised
I didn't talk for a year and a half.
—Gracie Allen

I have two birthdays. For eighteen years, I celebrated September 2 as my birthday. I figured since my mom was there, she had to have known when I was born.

But apparently there was some confusion. According to my birth certificate, which I sent away for when I turned eighteen, I was born on September 1, not 2. I could understand the discrepancy if my birth had taken place around midnight, but according to the certificate I arrived much earlier in the day on the first.

Still, I can't blame my mom for the mix-up. I was the last of five children, so I'm sure by then she was pretty tired. The fact that she knew it was the month of September is probably good enough. Besides, now I get to celebrate both the first and the second, so it works out kind of nice; especially if someone forgets to call, they get a second chance.

Birthdays are important. They're the anniversary of the day when we first came into this world, took a single gasp of air, and screamed at the top of our lungs to let everyone within earshot know that we were here and it was time to party!

As we grew, most of us continued having a great time. We didn't worry about the grocery bill while sitting there in our high chair eating chocolate cupcakes and asking for more. We didn't think twice about the state of the economy as we played with our toys or colored in our coloring books. The rising cost of gasoline and car insurance never even entered our minds as we rode our tricycle around the patio or dared to take that first ride on a two-wheeler.

Then came school. This was an adjustment. We had to start balancing fun with work. There were tests and homework and science projects and books to read before we could even think about doing anything fun.

Our first job reinforced this thought, too. We were learning the concept of earning money to pay for whatever fun we were having. We were also discovering that someone else had been footing the bill for our fun all our life. Now it was our turn to step up to the plate and start paying our own way.

Marriage brought us even more responsibilities, more bills, and longer hours at work. We still tried to make time for fun, but it wasn't as easy now. How could we spend an evening just laughing and having fun when there were so many other, more important things to do?

The birth of our children brought some of that carefree fun back into our lives. But often as an onlooker. We could watch our kids playing with their toys or riding their two-wheelers, but we were too busy writing checks for our monthly credit card payments. We knew we'd have more fun later, but right then all we really wanted to do was get a good night's sleep.

And so, here we are. Our kids are grown. The toys (our own and our children's) are all packed away, or we sold them at a garage sale. We have a lot more time on our hands for fun, but unfortunately, by now too many of us have lost our sense of humor. The weight of all the years of responsibilities, bills, disappointments, hurts, and troubles has pressed down on us for so long, we don't remember what it was like to enjoy life.

When we were young, no one had to tell us to have fun. We just did it, remember? We could play with a string for hours, skip a rock along a stream, fly kites, swing on a swing at the park, tell jokes, write funny notes to a friend, build something out of nothing, watch our favorite TV shows. Whatever we did, we made it fun. We enjoyed it to the fullest. Sometimes we even had more fun with the box a toy came in than we did with the toy itself.

So how do we find that spirit of fun again? We simply let it out. It's been inside us all along.

God writes a lot of comedy . . . the trouble is,
he's stuck with so many bad actors who
don't know how to play funny.
—Garrison Keillor

45

Ten Things to Do the Day You Retire

1. Conduct a memorial service for your alarm clock.
2. Have another memorial service ten minutes later for the snooze alarm.
3. Clean out your desk and find every item that you had reported lost over the last twenty years.
4. Turn in your company key. (Now that you found it and four copies in your desk drawer.)
5. Plant hydrangeas in your lunch pail.
6. Build a business card bonfire and roast marshmallows.
7. Write your boss a letter telling him how much he or she has meant to you over the years.
8. Tear up the above letter, and write another one that you can actually give him or her.

9. Review your financial situation, determining how long you can stay retired before you have to go out and look for another job.
10. Look for another job.

46

Another Way to Look at It

You know, somebody actually complimented me on my driving today. They left a little note on the windscreen, it said "Parking Fine."
—Tommy Cooper

What if age spots were considered beauty marks and wrinkles were something you asked a plastic surgeon to add, instead of take away? Imagine a world where every birthday was looked forward to with as much excitement and anticipation as your twenty-first. What if rocking chairs were as hip as Harleys and baggy skin was chic? What if we were able to turn society's opinion of the over-forty crowd around to where middle-agers were looked upon with envy?

"Oooh, she just got her first liver spot. It's not fair! She always gets everything before I do!"

"Look at her over there, flaunting her cellulite. I bet it's not even real."

"I'm going to the Tan and Wilt. You know how I like to get a head start on my wrinkled look before summer gets here."

"What's wrong with me? I'm in my thirties and gravity hasn't set in yet. I feel like a freak!"

Don't think it will ever happen? Look at how the public's attitude toward cigarette smoking has changed. Remember when non-smoking sections used to be two broken-down booths in the back of restaurants? Then it grew to half the restaurant, then the whole restaurant, and now in some states, there's a no-smoking policy in all public places.

So how do we go about changing the public's perception of the over-forty crowd? One thing we can do is convince more national magazines to feature pretty middle-aged women and well-toned middle-aged men on their covers. In their interviews, middle-aged entertainers can refer to their liver spots as beauty marks and talk about their hot flashes with the same enthusiasm as they would a trip to Cannes.

We can book great-looking representatives of our age group on all the talk shows, and show before-and-after pictures featuring the blandness of perfect skin next to the amazing character of aging skin.

When you get down to it, what's so great about smooth, taut skin anyway? Wrinkles tell stories. What stories does a twenty-year-old face have to tell? It may be pretty, but there is no history, no back story. I, on the other hand, have an entire novel written on my face. On some mornings, it's a trilogy.

So let's all do our part. Let's make the world wish they were one of us. We've got what they really want down deep inside. We've just got to let them know it.

**Beautiful young people are accidents of nature,
but beautiful old people are works of art.**
—Eleanor Roosevelt

47

Advantages to Aging

❁ You can use PoliGrip to repair broken knickknacks.

❁ You can fall asleep during an hour-and-a-half sermon and people will assume you're praying.

❁ You can drive the median on the highway and avoid the traffic.

❁ You get to take advantage of those senior discounts.

❁ People hold the doors open for you, which usually gets you in line in front of them.

❁ You can answer your grandchildren's history questions with firsthand accounts of your childhood.

❁ People let you be cranky.

❁ You can turn up the television set louder than your grandson's stereo.

❁ Three sit-ups count as exercise.

❁ You can walk down the street talking to yourself, with or without a headset.

48

Bookkeeping 101

Have you had a kindness shown? Pass it on;
'twas not given for thee alone, Pass it on;
Let it travel down the years,
Let it wipe another's tears,
Till in Heaven the deed appears, Pass it on.
—Henry Burton

It's important for us to keep good records of our debts. I'm not talking about debts to Visa, MasterCard, or others who not-so-freely gave to you, then charged outrageous interest rates while you've paid them back over a mere twenty or thirty years. Those debts are easy to keep track of and hard to escape.

I'm talking about emotional debts, kindness debts, friend-ship debts, and the huge debt we owe those who have fought and continue to fight for the freedoms we all enjoy. We owe a debt to our parents, who sacrificed so we can have what they never had; to our teachers who spent extra time with us helping us realize our own potential; and of course, to our faithful friends who were there for us when we needed them most. That's why *It's A Wonderful Life* is such an inspirational movie. George Bailey's friends remembered their debts. They remembered how much they owed George for his past kindnesses. They owed him their loyalty. They owed him their faith in his goodness. They didn't walk out when he needed them most. The people of Bedford Falls kept good record of their debts.

Too many of us don't keep good books. We forget the favors paid to us, the kindnesses shown to us, the good advice given us, and the love bestowed on us. We forget a lot.

I'll be the first to admit that I'm in debt up to my eyeballs with people. I owe my personal freedoms to every uniformed man or woman, soldier, police officer, and other peacekeepers who have ever fought for our country or put their own safety at risk so I can sleep peacefully at night.

I owe another enormous debt to my parents, who worked tirelessly to make sure there was food on the table and a roof over our heads. I'm the youngest of five children, and while my parents certainly had their challenges, and we weren't rich by any stretch of the imagination, I cannot ever remember going to bed hungry or cold.

I'm also in debt to my friends who have stood by me in good times and difficult times, who've been rocks of encouragement, saying just the right things at just the right times. I wouldn't want to think what my life would be like without them.

I owe my children a huge debt, too, for blessing me more than they'll ever know simply by being in my life. Through them, I've learned to trust God, believe in his perfect timing, and understand his loving fatherly qualities. Knowing how we want the best for our children helps us understand how God wants the best for us.

I owe a debt to those who have in any way encouraged me in my writing—so many family members, pastors, editors, friends, English teachers, and especially the person who wrote to me saying that he found one of my articles in a trashcan, liked it, and wondered if I had written any books. (I wrote back telling him that I had and which trashcans he might find some of them in, too.) Writing has always been my passion, and thanks to so many, and especially you who are buying the books, it has become my livelihood.

I owe a debt to every person who has ever made me laugh. Professional comedians such as Jackie Gleason, Bob Hope, Jerry Lewis, Steve Martin, Jerry Seinfeld, Dick Van Dyke, the entire cast of *Everybody Loves Raymond,* and so many others. And the non-professionals, just everyday people who have shared laughs over lunches, business meetings, parties, or who simply sent a note or a funny thought to make me smile.

I even owe a debt to those whom I've encountered through-out my life who haven't been so kind, perhaps even downright nasty. We've all had people like this cross our path, but they can teach us a great deal, too. If nothing else, they can show us how *not* to treat others.

So, yes, I am in debt. I am up to my eyeballs in debt. And the debt just keeps growing. Every day I become indebted to someone else who has graced my life with their kind words or encouragement.

I hope, too, that I'm listed in other people's records for

whatever kindnesses I've shown to them. That's what life is all about—remembering our debts. Remembering those who have helped us, sacrificed for us, inspired us, and loved us for who we are. Life is a combination of laughter and tears, good times and not-so-good times, encouragers and discouragers, for they have all made us who we are.

We all have bad days, we all have disappointments, we all have to deal with unkind people, but if we are honest with ourselves, truly honest, we would have to admit that there are a lot more people on the positive side of our balance sheets than on the negative side. The problem is we just forget to make the entries.

When it comes to life, be an accurate bookkeeper.

By the time you're eighty years old
you've learned everything.
You only have to remember it.
—George Burns

49

Caretakers

*There's so much pollution in the air now
that if it weren't for our lungs
there'd be no place to put it all.*
—Robert Orben

What if the world were a library book that we had to check out
at our birth, then turn back in just before our death? How
much do you think we'd be fined for the condition in which
we're returning it?

Don't get me wrong. I'm sure the majority of us don't want
to purposely hurt the earth. We want to protect its beauty and
even improve it so those who follow after us will enjoy the
fruits of our progress. But progress, good as it is, comes at a
price.

Automobiles have made getting to work much easier, but
they have also been a major contributor to pollution.

The telephone made it possible for us to communicate with
loved ones and business associates all over the world. But now

with cell phones in such abundance, we find ourselves listening to everyone's private conversations wherever we go. (Aren't you amazed at how many people will sit at McDonald's or Burger King and discuss company takeovers, unsatisfactory employees, and other delicate business affairs within earshot of everyone around them? We're going to have fast-food workers going from "You want fries with that?" to running multi-million dollar companies thanks to the education they're receiving from eavesdropping on CEOs for free.)

The Internet, which enables us to reach almost any company or person in the world, was another terrific idea. But the Internet also enables almost any company or person in the world to reach us with an endless bombardment of spam. And don't forget about the identity thefts.

Another idea that someone of our generation came up with is credit cards. Think of the convenience! Think of the opportunity! Think of the 22 percent interest! It has been estimated that the average credit card debt now carried by American families is around $9,000. Sure, credit cards seemed like a good idea when they first came out, but things have gotten out of hand when they're sending two-year-olds those "Congratulations, you're already approved!" letters. I'm sorry, but two-year-olds don't need an American Express or a MasterCard. One Visa card is enough.

Television was from our generation, too. We can now get the news as soon as it happens. The downside? We can now get the news as soon as it happens. Sometimes even before it's verified for authenticity. They also give us every sordid detail of news stories that aren't even adult friendly, much less child friendly. What all this information, speculation, innuendo, and sometimes even fabrication is doing to us as a society is yet to be fully determined. We'll find out, I suppose, when we check in our "library book" at the end of our watch.

The advances we've made in medical research have given us antibiotics to combat all sorts of diseases. Unfortunately, because of our own misuse of them, we now have smarter viruses that are mutating and becoming less susceptible to our "miracle drugs."

Our advances in DNA studies have given us amazing crime-solving abilities and fast-tracked us on the path toward cures for many life-threatening diseases. But it has also given us the moral dilemma of cloning.

Progress. It comes at a price.

So how will our "library book" be handed back in? Will it be tattered and ripped and stained from our not having taken very good care of it? Or will we be turning in a book that we've not only enjoyed every page of, but one that's in even better condition than when it was first handed to us? The answer is up to us.

I'm moving to Mars next week,
so if you have any boxes . . .
—Steven Wright

50

Sending My Regrets

*Someday we'll look back on this moment
and plow into a parked car.*
—Evan Davis

We all have them. Those memories that make us shudder.

Those times when we think, *What in the world was I thinking?*

Those days when we mentally beat ourselves up over why we didn't do this or did do that. You know, all those could'ves, should'ves, and would'ves of life. They're called regrets, and who among us doesn't have some?

I regret that perm I got when I was a teenager. But at least this year the curl finally relaxed.

I regret not having the foresight to have invested in IBM.

I regret not having taken a picture of my Popeye arms after my upper-arm fat avalanche. (But I do at least have medical documentation.)

Other regrets, though, are a little harder for us to live with.

Regret that we didn't spend enough time with that loved one before he passed. Regret that we didn't stand up for a friend when she needed our support. Regret that we didn't do enough, give enough, go enough, or be enough.

We certainly can't erase our past regrets, but we can do something about minimizing any future ones. If you believe that one day you're going to regret not having spent enough time with your children, spouse, parents, friends, or any other loved one, then start spending more time with them now.

If you're going to regret not having thanked someone for something they did for you, even if it was years ago, thank them now.

If you're going to regret not having used your talents more, start using them now.

If you're going to regret not having saved more of your money, then start saving more now.

If you're going to regret not having seen more of the world, then start traveling now. Even if you can't afford to travel to far-away places, take in some weekend trips. There are plenty of places of interest to visit right here at home.

If you're going to regret not having spoken up for someone who couldn't speak up for herself, then speak up now.

If you're going to regret not having chosen to do the right thing more often, then start choosing to do the right thing now.

Regrets. You'll only have as many as you allow yourself to have.

You can't keep blaming yourself.
Just blame yourself once, and move on.
—Homer Simpson

51

Top Twenty Things That You Might Have Been Looking For When You Couldn't Remember What It Was You Were Looking For

1. checkbook
2. sweater
3. glasses
4. paper
5. pen
6. wallet
7. magazine
8. address book

9. tape
10. cell phone
11. medicine
12. towel
13. candy
14. purse
15. calculator
16. shoes
17. paper clip
18. husband
19. pet
20. the right house

52

Survivor

The hardest years in life are
those between ten and seventy.
—Helen Hayes

No matter how much you wish you didn't have to accept it, no
one gets through this life without realizing one very basic
truth—the journey isn't perfect. We can wish for it to be perfect, we can hope and pray that it will be perfect, we can live in
denial thinking it is perfect. But despite all our good efforts, it
is more likely that we'll have a lot of failures and successes,
hurts and healings, plans and adjustments, fulfilled dreams and
forgotten ones.

So what do we do? How do we survive this thing called life?
We learn to partake of the four basic attitudes every day.

Appreciate

Adjust

Persevere

Celebrate

Each day of your life should have a healthy serving from every one of these groups.

Appreciate. This is where many of us struggle the most. When things go wrong, it's easy to allow the current crisis to partially or completely block the good in our life from our field of vision. We focus on our trials and forget our treasures. We see our problems and ignore our pearls. But to truly appreciate life, we have to look at the whole picture.

Adjust. Life is about making adjustments. Rewriting the script of our lives as we live it. It's about changes—some planned, others unexpectedly thrust upon us. Sometimes life goes in the exact opposite direction of what we wanted. We may have had dreams of our son going to West Point, but he decided he'd rather work at Wiener Hut (he thinks their hats are "way cooler"). The daughter we groomed to enter the medical field entered rehab instead. The child we hoped to send to Yale is now living in a commune outside of Phoenix. What happened? Simple. A parent's dreams met a child's choices.

If we did our best, all we can do is hope and pray, leave the outcome in God's hands, and . . .

Persevere. Why? Because we have to. And not just for ourselves. We persevere for those around us. When we make it through a problem, others look for a little residual hope to help them make it through their problem, too.

And because we persevere, we can . . .

Celebrate. We're alive and that is more than enough reason to party! We survived all the times when we didn't know where our next meal was coming from. We survived that night when we didn't think our son or daughter was going to make it through their latest crisis. We survived that day when the world was filled with uncertainty and none of us, not even our leaders, knew what was going to happen next. We survived that job loss, that surgery, that car accident, that earthquake, that hurricane, that tornado, that stock-market adjustment. We've survived it all. And chances are we'll survive a lot more before this ride is over.

So remember the four life groups—appreciate, adjust, persevere, and celebrate. Are you getting enough of each of these in your daily diet?

The answer to old age is to keep one's mind busy and to go on with one's life as if it were interminable. I always admired Chekhov for building a new house when he was dying of tuberculosis.
—Leon Edel

53

What Was That?

Have you ever had something flash across your field of vision, but since you weren't really paying attention, you didn't get a good look at what it was?

"Hey, what was that?" you might have said to whomever was standing by you at the time, hoping they caught a better glimpse of it than you did. All you know is something went whooshing by, but as to what it was, you don't have a clue.

If we're not careful, that's what we'll be saying about our lives someday.

"What was that?" we'll ask. "Did you see what just flew by? I didn't get a good look at it, but I think it might have been my life."

We've all been reminded umpteen times how fleeting life is, but how much do we really believe it? We certainly didn't believe it in our teens. We were in too much of a hurry to graduate high school or get to our twenty-first birthday to think about the downside of rushing through our years.

In our twenties and thirties we were too busy pursuing our careers, building our families, and going after our dreams to notice how quickly the calendar pages were being turned. We kept up that frantic pace until we finally passed the middle-age marker, and now time is passing so quickly, we're begging someone to help us put on the brakes. Or better yet, shift to reverse.

But life doesn't work that way. It only has one gear, and that's forward. How quickly or how slowly we move ahead in that gear is up to us.

It's not easy, though. We get caught up in the daily struggles of our existence—financial worries, traffic jams, crowded malls, rude waiters, pushy neighbors, manipulative people, insensitive bosses—all the things that can and do consume much more of our time than we realize or want. Before we know it, we've wasted a week dwelling on this problem, two weeks worrying about that problem, or even a year or more nursing an old wound. If we're not careful, the people and problems that deserve the least amount of our time end up taking the most of our time. Time that, no matter how hard we try, we are never going to get back.

Let me ask you, are you making the kind of memories you want to have at the end of your life? Do you hold up those car payment receipts with the same enthusiasm as you would hold a photo of you and your family vacationing in Nantucket? Is the picture of you sitting at your computer as exciting as one would be of you landing a big catch off the Florida coast? Are you happy with the way you are spending your time?

"You don't understand. I've got my SUV payment, my credit card bills, the mortgage, my cable bill. Someday I'll take a vacation, but I just can't do it this year."

But next year rolls around and you can't afford to take one then either. And the next year. And the next. Before you know it, more of your life has just whooshed by and you have nothing more to show for it.

Maybe it's time we all revisited our day planners. Maybe it's time we finally admitted to ourselves that the days and weeks we're spending now on whatever we're spending them on won't be coming back. Maybe it's time we treated our spouses and our children, our parents and our friends as more valuable commodities than stocks, bank accounts, or social standing.

Yesterday is what it was. All we have is today and tomorrow. From birth to middle age to our senior years, it's up to us to live our lives to the fullest, to not give others the power to decide how happy, how satisfied, or how fulfilled we're going to feel. Too many of us aren't living the life we want to live because we're living someone else's dreams, or we're chained to debt, or we've committed to things that our heart just isn't in, and now we feel trapped, or we've allowed others to steal our joy.

So take a moment and ask yourself, what is it that is most important to you? Is whatever it is high on your priority list right now, or does your priority list need a rewrite?

It's up to each one of us to live every day, every hour, every minute of our lives so that when we get to the end, we won't have to say "What was that? Did you see what just flew by? I didn't get a good look at it, but I think it was my life."

Each day comes bearing its own gifts.
Untie the ribbons.
—Ruth Ann Schabacker